Kieler Studien

Institut für Weltwirtschaft an der Universität Kiel

Herausgegeben von Herbert Giersch

145

Charles R. Chittle, Ph. D.

Industrialization and Manufactured Export Expansion in a Worker-Managed Economy

The Yugoslav Experience

J.C.B. MOHR (PAUL SIEBECK) TÜBINGEN

ISSN 0340-6989

CIP-Kurztitelaufnahme der Deutschen Bibliothek

Chittle, Charles R.
Industrialization and manufactured export expansion in a worker-managed economy: the Yugoslav experience. — 1. Aufl. — Tübingen: Mohr, 1977.
(Kieler Studien; 145)
ISBN 3-16-339671-2 kart.
ISBN 3-16-339672-0 Lw.

Schriftleitung: Hubertus Müller-Groeling

Printed in Germany
ISSN 0340-6989

To my wife and my parents

Contents

Page

Page

List of Figures

List of Tables

Page

Statistical Appendix

Preface

The theme of this book is the foreign trade and industrialization policies of the labor-managed economy of Yugoslavia. The study is part of a larger research project of the Institut für Weltwirtschaft, Kiel, dealing with import substitution and export diversification in fifteen developing countries. Research for the entire project has been carried out under the auspices of "Sonderforschungsbereich 86, Weltwirtschaft und internationale Wirtschaftsbeziehungen (Kiel/Hamburg)", with financial support provided by the Deutsche Forschungsgemeinschaft.

Although the institutional basis of the Yugoslav economy is unique, useful lessons can be learned from an examination of the industrial development of the country. Rapid economic growth has been achieved coincident with frequent institutional change. Policies of import substitution and manufactured export expansion have been pursued simultaneously. Yugoslavia is now one of the leading exporters of manufactured goods among the developing nations. And while no other country has adopted workers' self-management on the scale that Yugoslavia has, the world-wide trend is to give workers more influence in the operation of business firms.

My debts are many. Going back to my undergraduate days at Hiram college, Gene Andress and T.O. Weir, my first economics teachers, provided the inspiration and encouragement to pursue my study of economics at the graduate level. At Purdue University, Jay Wiley provided valuable guidance and counseling, while M. June Flanders, my dissertation supervisor, immeasurably contributed to my training in the art of research. I also would like to express my gratitude to Bowling Green State University for granting me a leave of absence so that I could spend two years abroad.

A huge debt is owed to the Institut für Weltwirtschaft for providing me with the financial support and extraordinary facilities and environment to engage in this research. The President of the Institut, Herbert Giersch, in addition to being the primary factor behind the above conditions, was helpful in making it possible for me to travel to Yugoslavia in connection with my research. Juergen Donges, the head of the development economics department at the Institut and co-director of the research project, gave me full freedom of development of my research while at the same time offering valuable substantive and organizational advice. My special thanks go to Richard Pomfret for his incisive comments made in the course of our daily "Arbeitspause".

Juergen Donges' and Richard Pomfret's meticulous reading of an earlier draft and their perceptive comments were of great help to me, as well as James Riedel's comments on parts of the study. I also benefited from discussions with J. P. Agarwal, Ranadev Banerji, Maurice Girgis, Ulrich Hiemenz, Dieter Lotz, Ghazy Mujahid, Lotte Müller-Ohlsen, Bernd Stecher, William Tyler and Peter Wogart.

Julia Feldmeier professionally, cheerfully and swiftly typed various versions of the study. Her competence lightened my burdens. Statistical help was ably provided by Klaus Zanzig, Lilian Ebel, Ingeborg Mattscherodt and Brigitte Paulus. Numerous members of the library staff at the Institut were very helpful. I am especially grateful to Milija Pajević for translation assistance and information on the Yugoslav literature, data sources, institutions and economists. I also owe much to Milan Aleksić and Mihailov Jovanović for their assistance during my field work in Yugoslavia. Others to whom I am thankful for various reasons include Ingrid Hohmann and several Yugoslav economists. Thanks are also due to Ursula Wollesen for meticulously preparing the manuscript for publication.

My deepest gratitude is to my wife, Ani, for help in all aspects of the preparation of the manuscript.

Any errors and omissions are, of course, the sole responsibility of the author.

Bowling Green, Ohio, July 1976 Charles R. Chittle

Chapter I: Introduction

Yugoslavia is the world's only self-managed economy. Not only has workers' self-management been more extensively adopted at the business enterprise level in Yugoslavia than elsewhere, but self-management pervades all aspects of the life of the country. The nation has also achieved a growth rate of the national product during the last three decades that ranks among the world's highest. While Yugoslavia's unique economic system has been examined from various angles, there has been, to this author's knowledge, no comprehensive analysis of the international economic policies of this innovative economy. This study aims at filling the gap, with major emphasis being devoted to examining the role of manufactured export expansion in the achievement of rapid industrial growth in a self-managed system. In this chapter, the main elements of the worker-managed system are described. Then follows an explanation of why a case study of Yugoslav industrialization and international economic policies is important.

1. The Labor-Managed Enterprise

The legal basis of the workers' self-management system in Yugoslavia was established in 1950 with the passage of the Basic Law on the Management of Economic Enterprises and Higher Economic Associations by the Working Collectives. However, the system was not actually operational until 1952. A process of experimentation and change has been taking place ever since. The general trend of the past two decades has been toward greater political and economic decentralization, greater reliance on the market and an enlargement of the decision-making power of the enterprises. The autonomy of the enterprise, except on decisions regarding what and how much to produce, was severely limited prior to the reforms of the 1960s.

a. Governance in the Worker-Managed Enterprise

Workers' self-management and economic decentralization grew out of the Yugoslav rejection of the Soviet model of centralized economic organization. The economic grounds for turning away from central planning include the argument that such a system is useful during the initial stage of development but becomes a burden as the development process takes hold. There was a feeling that étatism resulted in state bureaucrats replacing capitalists as exploiters of the workers. A unique feature of the establishment of workers' management in Yugoslavia is that, in contrast to movements in this direction taken in other countries, the initiating force came from above rather than from the workers themselves.

While workers' self-management is not a Yugoslav invention, it has been adopted on a much wider scale there than elsewhere and is the cornerstone of the Yugoslav socio-economic system. Although the concern of this study is limited to workers' self-management in business enterprises, the concept of self-management in Yugoslavia has spread to other institutions, e.g., universities, hospitals, libraries, research institutes and other social and public services. The private sector, consisting mainly of agriculture and services, is exempt from the rule of self-management[1]. This sector contributed 18.9 percent of Yugoslavia's social product in 1973[2].

The Yugoslav business firm is neither privately nor state owned but is "socially owned". Social ownership is a legal concept and means that the firm is owned by society as a whole, while the use of the property is granted to the employees. Prior to its abolishment in 1971, a tax was levied on the firm's assets (the maximum rate was 6 percent). Capital assets of the enterprise may be sold; however, the proceeds must be reinvested and cannot be distributed as personal income. Management of the socially owned property is vested in the employees of the enterprise, that is, the workers' collective. The workers' council is elected by the workers' collective; it consists of 15 to 120 members, depending upon the size of the enterprise[3]. The council performs a policy-making function: it adopts economic plans and by-laws of the enterprise, elects members of the management board, decides on the distribution of the net earnings of the enterprise, sets wage norms and rules on matters concerning joint ventures and mergers.

---

[1] The private sector in agriculture accounts for about 85 percent of the cultivated land. Private holdings are limited to 10 hectares per family. The private sector accounted for 75 percent of agricultural value-added in 1973.

[2] Social product, or gross material product, is similar to gross national product; it excludes certain "non-productive" activities such as government administration, education, health and personal services. Social product is about 15 percent less than gross national product defined according to Western definitions.

[3] Enterprises are free to fix the tenure and size of the council in their by-laws. In enterprises of up to 30 employees, the workers' council consists of all the workers. The average workers' council consists of 20-25 members.

The management board, elected by the workers' council, is responsible for more detailed, day-to-day operations. This board usually consists of 5 to 11 members elected by the workers' council from among its members, with the exception of the enterprise director, who is an ex officio member of the board but is not a member of the council. The board acts like an executive arm of the council; it draws up the production plans, prepares financial reports and various proposals for the council, executes council decisions and supervises the direction of the enterprise. Three-fourths of the members of the board must be production workers[1].

The enterprise director is appointed by the workers' council from applicants considered on the basis of public competition. His term of office is four years with reelection and early dismissal possible. His functions are specified in the by-laws of the enterprise and include supervising and coordinating the firm's operations and carrying out decisions of the workers' council and management board.

When the workers' self-management system was first put into practice, the enterprises actually had little decision-making power concerning the distribution of their net income, i.e., gross income less non-labor costs. The trend over time has been for the share of income that the enterprise has free distribution of to rise; this discretionary income currently amounts to over 70 percent of the net income of industrial enterprises. Important relaxation of controls over the enterprises occured as part of the economic reform of 1965. A major motivation behind this action was to improve economic efficiency; a key part of the reform relating to the enterprises was the grant-

[1] Members of the board and council are protected from dismissal or transfer. In the larger enterprises self-management has been decentralized so that, in addition to the workers' council and management board of the entire enterprise, separate self-management bodies exist at, for example, the plant or process levels. These Basic Organizations of Associated Labor (BOAL) are now evolving as the basic decision-making unit in the economic sphere. This decentralization of enterprise operations is consistent with the Constitution of 1974. Each unit of an enterprise which produces a product (or service) that can technically be marketed can form its own BOAL. Decisions on such matters as income distribution, hiring and firing, job assignments and working conditions may be made at the BOAL level of self-management. A BOAL may also disassociate itself from an enterprise and form an autonomous enterprise or join another enterprise. Joint decision-making among two or more BOALs may occur. The enterprise by-laws specify those decision-making powers that are vested in the enterprise (central) workers' council and those belonging to the work unit councils. About 16 percent of the enterprises had more than one workers' council in 1972. Most enterprises have

ing of permission to them to decide on the distribution of their net income between a wage fund and other funds[1]. The firms have maintained autonomy in such areas as what, how much, and how to produce. There nevertheless is a question regarding the real autonomy of the Yugoslav enterprise. The director of the enterprise has invariably been a member of the Yugoslav League of Communists. The extent of the League's influence on enterprise operations through its members on the management board and workers' council as well as the directorship is difficult to ascertain and is a topic beyond the scope of this paper[2]. The view here is that the director's allegiance is to the enterprise rather than the League. There also is discussion about the extent to which workers actually participate in management decisions. The degree of participation varies between enterprises; in some firms the director is very strong, in others the workers operating through the workers' council are more influential[3].

b. The Theory of the Worker-Managed Enterprise

The pioneering work on the theory of the worker-managed firm was done by Benjamin Ward [1958][4]. Further theoretical developments were made by Domar [1966], Rockwell [1968], Vanek [1970] and Horvat [1967][5]. Vanek has developed a comprehensive theory of a labor-managed economy. Only the bare elements of the operating principles of a worker-managed enterprise will be examined in this study. The reader interested in a thorough analysis is referred to the above sources.

Ward posited that a rational worker-managed firm would seek to maximize net income (= gross income less non-labor costs, i.e., wages plus profits in familiar capitalist terminology) per worker (Y). This operating principle, referred to by Vanek [1970, p. 2] as "natural and

---

elected in recent years to dispense with the management board. The director in this case chooses unofficial advisors who have no decision-making authority.

[1] Some retreat in the relaxation of controls over enterprises has since taken place.

[2] For further information see: Milenkovitch [1971, Chapter 5].- Dirlam, Plummer [1973, Chapter 3].- Wachtel [1973, Chapter 5].

[3] See, for example, Obradović [1975]. - The rise in the importance of the BOAL that is currently taking place can be seen as strengthening self-management and emphasizing the role of the individual worker while reducing the power of top management of the enterprise.

[4] Developed further in Ward [1967, Chapters 8-10].

[5] For additional works on the economics of the worker-managed firm see Furubotn, Pejovich [1973]. - Furubotn [1971, 1976]. - Maurice, Ferguson [1972].

rational" leads to different operating conditions of the worker-managed firm as compared to a capitalist firm. Consider first the simple case of a firm employing two inputs: a fixed input, capital (K) and a variable input, labor (L). Assume the existence of pure competition in all markets, homogeneous and divisible factors of production and eventually diminishing returns. The firm will employ labor up to the point where the net income per worker is equal to the marginal value product of labor. Employing labor beyond this point would lower the income of existing employees and thus would be irrational. The equilibrium situation is illustrated in Figures 1 and 2[1], where the notation is as follows:

L	= number of employees
X	= quantity of output
P_X	= price of output
K_O	= quantity of capital
P_K	= price of capital
MVP_L	= marginal value product of labor
AVP_L	= average value product of labor
Y	= net income per worker = $\frac{P_X X - P_K K_O}{L}$

Equilibrium occurs at points e with L_E of labor employed.

At the equilibrium position $MVP_L = Y$. That this will be the case is seen in Figure 2, where the slope of ae (= Y) is at a maximum when ae is tangent to $P_X X$. The slope of $P_X X = MVP_L$. Thus at maximum Y, $Y = MVP_L$[2]. This is analogous to the employment decision of a profit-maximizing capitalist firm which employs labor up to the point where the wage rate equals MVP_L. A resource allocation problem

---

[1] Adopted from Vanek [1970, pp. 21 sq.].

[2] Sacks [1973, pp. 31 sq.] has demonstrated the equality of Y and MVP_L mathematically. Using the same terminology as above, $Y = \frac{P_X X - P_K K}{L}$. Differentiating Y with respect to L and setting this equal to zero (P_X, P_K and K are constants), yields $L = \frac{P_X X - P_K K}{P_X \frac{dX}{dL}}$. Substituting the latter expression into the former results in $Y = P_X \frac{dX}{dL} = MVP_L$.

Figure 1 - Short-Run Equilibrium of the Enterprise: 1

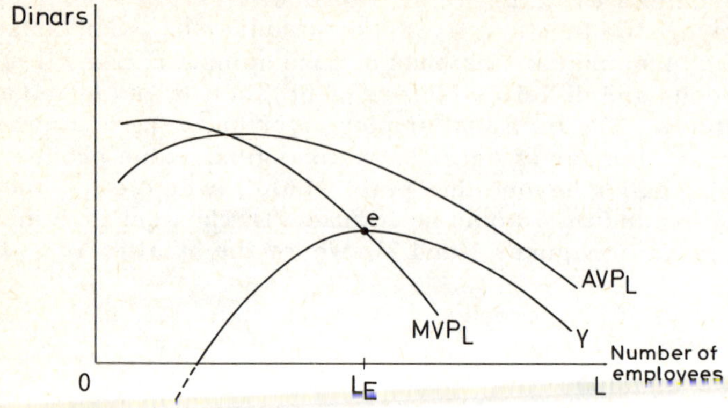

Figure 2 - Short-Run Equilibrium of the Enterprise: 2

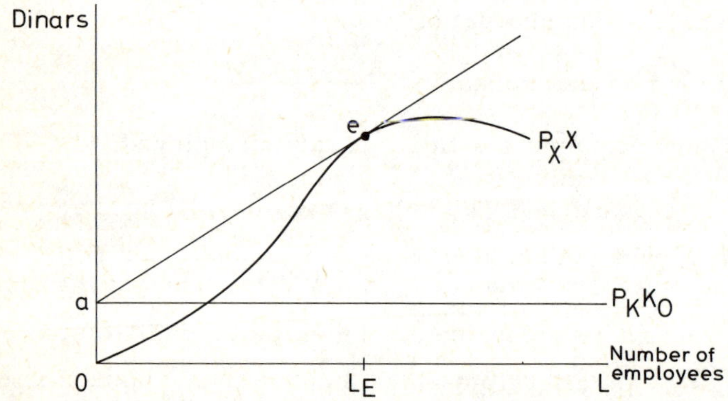

exists in the worker-managed economy to the extent that the net income curves differ between firms. Given the existence of different Ys, MVP_L will not be equalized among firms in the short run.

The operating principle of the worker-managed enterprise also leads to the employment of factors of production in proportions different from those in the capitalist firm. In this connection three cases can be distinguished:

A. The wage rate (W) faced by the capitalist firm is less than the net income per worker (Y) of the worker-managed firm
B. W = Y
C. W > Y

In case A, W < Y implies the capitalist firm is making positive profits. This would seem to be the more common situation. Employing labor to the point where the wage rate is equal to the marginal value product of labor obviously results in greater employment than would exist in the worker-managed firm employing labor up to the point where the higher net income per worker equals the marginal value product. Consequently, the worker-managed enterprise will use a more capital-intensive technology. The analysis of cases B and C is similar. The factor proportions would be identical in the former case and in C they would be the opposite of A[1].

The comparison of factor proportions in the worker-managed and capitalist firm in the long run is more complex. The conclusions, however, are in line with those reached in the previous short-run analysis. The tendency is for the worker-managed firm to adopt a more capital-intensive (= less labor-intensive) technology[2]. Vanek [1970, p. 383] concludes that a competitive worker-managed firm will always operate at the point of maximum physical efficiency. Furthermore, in a dynamic situation where additions to the firm's capital stock are occuring, the size of worker-managed firms will be smaller and the capital/labor ratio higher as compared to an otherwise identical capitalist firm with positive profits[3]. The tendency of the worker-managed firm towards a smaller optimum size leads Vanek to conclude that markets will be more competitive under a system of workers' self-management [pp. 272-274]. An additional factor supporting the argument that a capital-intensive bias is a feature of workers' self-management is the likelihood that existing workers will not want their decision-making power to be diluted by the employment of additional workers.

c. Foreign Trade Implications

The capital-intensive bias of the worker-managed enterprise has two implications that are especially relevant to the present study. The

---

[1] Relaxing the assumption of two factors of production does not alter these conclusions regarding factor proportions. For an analysis of a four-input production model see Vanek [1970, pp. 23-27].

[2] The nature of the production function assumes importance here. For more on this, see Vanek [1970, pp. 27-34].

[3] For a more complete comparison of worker-managed and capitalist firms, e.g., differences in their reactions to changes in prices and costs, see the sources referred to on p. 4.

first conclusion to be drawn is that a system of workers' self-management does not provide for maximum employment creation[1]. This is especially important for capital-scarce developing countries with a large amount of unemployment or with a need to transfer labor from agriculture to industry. Second, compare the net income per worker with the wage rate paid by the capitalist firm making positive profits. The net income per worker being greater than the wage rate means that, in a labor-abundant country, worker management leads to relatively higher costs of production of labor-intensive goods than under capitalism. This can be seen in Figure 3.

Figure 3 - Factor Price Ratios and Relative Costs of Production

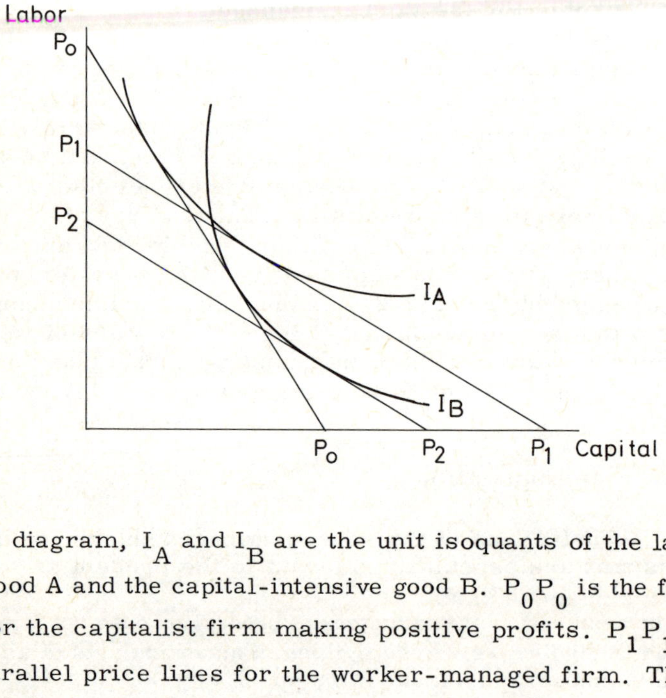

In this diagram, I_A and I_B are the unit isoquants of the labor-intensive good A and the capital-intensive good B. P_0P_0 is the factor price line for the capitalist firm making positive profits. P_1P_1 and P_2P_2 are parallel price lines for the worker-managed firm. The worker-

[1] This tendency may be mitigated by the relative ease of entry of new enterprises in Yugoslavia (view expressed by a Yugoslav economist in personal conversation). New enterprises may be founded by political bodies at all levels (federal, republic, local), social organizations, established enterprises and groups of citizens.

managed firms use a more capital-intensive process in both industries. In addition, per unit costs of A in relation to B are higher in the worker-managed economy. Thus, ceteris paribus, comparative advantage in labor-intensive goods is reduced as compared to the capitalist economy.

The theoretical analysis cannot, however, be applied unequivocally to the Yugoslav economy. Certain institutional factors must be brought into the analysis. In Yugoslavia the enterprise faces considerable pressure, e.g., from communes, to hire workers. It is also virtually impossible for workers to be dismissed. Yugoslav enterprises have been described by a Yugoslav economist as having redundant workers[1]. This observation by itself does not invalidate the theoretical conclusion that the worker-managed enterprise will adopt a relatively capital-intensive technology; capital may also be redundant. However, capital has been consistently underpriced in Yugoslavia. With real interest rates understating the scarcity of capital by a substantial margin, and the tax on fixed assets ranging from 2 to 6 percent until 1971, when the tax was abolished, abnormally high capital/labor ratios could be expected[2]. The underpricing of capital is also inconsistent with a desire to reduce the need for workers to emigrate.

Doubt about the capability of enterprises to follow the operating principle of maximizing net income per worker is increased by two additional considerations: 1) the level of advancement of the science of management in Yugoslav enterprises, and 2) the dynamic nature of the economic system as reflected in the frequent changes that occur in the system and the ability of enterprise management to keep up with the changes. The pioneering nature of the economic system has contributed to frequent institutional changes in the environment in which the firm operates. The changes have occurred at the internal firm level, e.g., the firm's autonomy over the distribution of its income, as well as at more macro levels, as will be revealed in following chapters. Thus it is a somewhat dubious proposition that the enterprise acts in the prescribed manner, even if it wanted to and were not constrained to do otherwise[3].

---

[1] Horvat [1971, p. 105]. - Since the mid-1960s the existence of redundant workers has become less common.

[2] See, e.g., Vanek [1973, pp. 42, 48].

[3] Additionally, a Yugoslav economist in personal conversation has suggested that the enterprise has different motives as between domestic and export sales. With respect to domestic sales, the goal is to maximize net income per worker. In so far as exports are concerned, the aim is to obtain foreign exchange so as to be able to import badly needed inputs regardless of the effect on income per worker.

Another feature of the workers' self-management system as it applies to Yugoslavia is worth noting for its possible effects on foreign trade. The system results in a compression of the spread between the minimum and maximum wages in an enterprise. This spread is now determined by extra-enterprise officials and varies between industries and areas; the maximum wage exceeds the minimum by a factor of only about 2.5-3[1]. This is surely a narrower spread than would be found in capitalist economies. An implication of this compression is that skilled workers are relatively underpaid when compared to unskilled workers. The country may be more internationally competitive in skilled labor-intensive goods than would be judged from a consideration of the relative physical abundance of skilled labor in Yugoslavia[2].

And finally factor mobility is negatively affected by institutional conditions. This in turn reduces the flexibility of the economy. Labor mobility is retarded by the stake in collective consumption, e.g., recreational facilities, that a worker acquires during the course of his employment in a specific enterprise[3]. In addition the worker obtains certain seniority benefits such as a better apartment (or his name moves higher up on the list for better housing). A conglomeration of non-pecuniary benefits also makes it difficult for the worker to compare his present total wage package with alternatives[4]. Capital mobility is restricted by the limited financial instruments and the regional orientation of the banks.

2. Commercial Policy and Industrialization: A Case Study of Yugoslavia

An important reason why the story of Yugoslavia's participation in the international division of labor during the course of rapid indus-

---

[1] The average personal income of the highest-paid university-educated workers was 2.73 times greater than the average income of the lowest-paid unskilled workers in 1966 [Gorupić, Paj 1970, p. 172].

[2] There is also some indication that the high priority given to education and training in Yugoslavia has led to an increase in highly educated and skilled personnel that outpaced the creation of positions consistent with such qualifications. Thus one study has found that unskilled labor is cheaper in Iran than in Yugoslavia, while the opposite relationship exists for more highly-skilled labor [Bildner 1973, pp. 45, 67].

[3] For more on this see Furubotn, Pejovich [1973, pp. 284 sq.].

[4] Ibid. - Another difficulty arises from the practice of not including income information in job advertisements.

trialization should be told centers around the country's unique self-management system. Other nations have some type of worker management but none has adopted a self-management system on anywhere near the scale of Yugoslavia's. Her experiences can thus provide useful information for other countries considering the adoption of a similar system. The lessons to be learned are all the more important in that there is a distinct world trend toward providing workers with increased participation in the operation of enterprises. This is so in both developing and developed countries[1].

A second reason why Yugoslavia provides an interesting case study of international economic policy and industrialization is the rapid growth rate that has been achieved. During 1952-1973 the social product grew at a compound annual rate of 7.6 percent, while industrial value added and manufactured exports grew at a rate of 10.5 and 12.0 percent respectively (in real terms) (Table 12). The industrialization of Yugoslavia has thus proceeded at an impressive pace, both by her own historical and by international standards. The international economic policies that have been pursued during the industrialization process deserve to be analyzed. Yugoslavia has now reached a stage of development that places the country in the semi-industrialized category. Thus the Yugoslav experience is worthy of study for the lessons it can provide for the many countries at lower stages of development. As a leader of the non-aligned bloc, Yugoslavia occupies an influential position among many of these countries.

As will be brought up in this study, Yugoslavia also provides a good example of a country that has simultaneously pursued policies of import substitution and export expansion. This is particularly remark-

---

[1] The following passage is indicative of current thought on this subject: "Elsewhere in the nine EEC countries the message has been unbelievably slow to get through but is now registering at last: the way to wed workers to capitalism, in sickness and health, is to put them in the boardroom and give them a part in running a firm's affairs ..." [The Economist]. (The 'elsewhere' refers to the exception of Germany, which moved in this direction in the 1950s.) While the type of worker participation foreseen here is a far cry from Yugoslavia's workers' self-management, it is indicative of the direction in which the world is moving. Peru is one of the developing countries which has already implemented a workers' participation system based on the philosophy of the Yugoslav model. A south European developing country, Portugal, is now considering adopting this model as well.

able in the background of the lasting discussion over inward-looking versus outward-looking growth strategies in developing countries[1]. Import-substituting industrialization policies were at the forefront in the 1950s. While this policy was not devoid of success, certain disappointments associated with the strategy have led, perhaps to some extent unjustifiably, to its having fallen into no small degree of disrepute. Among the defects and limitations that have been ascribed to the inward-looking strategy of import substitution are that it generates more imports than it saves (thus worsening the foreign exchange situation), leads to excessive costs and stifles efficiency incentives, does not generate sufficient employment, contributes to inflation, has undesirable effects on income distribution, and contributes to resource misallocation by discriminating against the primary and export sectors. Thus the 1960s ushered in the outward-looking strategy which would overcome many of the deficiencies of the previous misdirected policies. The new watchword became manufactured export promotion. The crutch of import substitution would be thrown aside and the patient would move proudly forward under his own steam. Efficiency would be stimulated, employment would expand more rapidly, and distortions of costs, prices and exchange rates would be minimized as specialization on the basis of comparative advantage was followed[2].

The position of this author is that, contrary to the manner in which the argument is frequently presented, there is little reason to think

---

[1] The various arguments (theoretical and empirical) in support of these (alternative?) strategies of industrialization have been well discussed in the literature and will not be gone into in detail here. See, for example, Streeten (Ed.) [1973]. - Little, Scitovsky, Scott [1970]. - Healey [1972]. - Keesing [1967]. - Bruton [1970]. - UNCTAD [1964b]. - Giersch (Ed.) [1974].

[2] The record fairly well speaks for itself in so far as the growth of manufactured exports of the developing countries is concerned. Exports of manufactures (SITC 5-8) from the developing countries grew at an annual compound rate of 15 percent during 1962-1972 (compared to a rate of less than 5 percent per annum during 1955-1962). The share of manufactured exports in total developing country exports reached 23 percent in 1972. Among the pace-setters in orienting manufacturing growth outwardly were Hong Kong, Singapore, Korea and Taiwan. Israel, Pakistan, Yugoslavia, Spain and Ireland were not far behind. Several countries in south and central America became more recent subscribers to the cause. Recent studies on manufactured export expansion include: Donges [1971]. - Donges, Riedel [1976]. - Pomfret [1975a]. - Chittle [1975b]. - Wogart [1975]. - Mujahid [1975]. - Müller-Ohlsen [1975]. - Riedel [1975b].

of import substitution and export promotion as "either/or" policies. While some period of import substitution may precede export promotion, there is no apparent reason why they cannot be pursued simultaneously[1]. Evidence in support of this view is contained in the present study. Thus there is other fodder for policy-makers to chew on. Import substitution industries are shown to have a relatively high import content of production, thus negating to a considerable extent the direct effects of the policy of import substitution. This result has promted one Yugoslav economist to describe the import substitution policy as a big failure. Export policy will be shown to have been more successful in achieving export growth than in following dictates of comparative advantage. As will be brought out later, major export industries have also had a high import requirement of production. Vast changes took place in the structure of aggregate as well as manufactured exports. Manufactured export growth exceeded the growth of industrial production. A further indication of manufactured export expansion is provided by the rise in the Yugoslav share of total developing country manufactured exports from 2.7 percent in 1955 to 9.4 percent in 1972. Policies permitting the outflow of emigrant workers from the country and the inflow of foreign capital in the form of direct investment, both bold steps for Yugoslavia to take, contain elements of both inward and outward-looking strategies.

A fourth reason for the relevance of a case study on Yugoslavia relates to her foreign investment policy. In addition to having been a pioneer in adopting the workers' self-management system on a large scale, Yugoslavia has been an innovator in attracting foreign capital. The foreign investment takes place in a form of contractual joint venture. The foreign partner does not gain ownership of any domestic property. The results of this experiment, especially concerning its effect on manufactured exports, are still rather primitive. Some preliminary conclusions are reached in a later chapter; it will be shown that inward-oriented foreign investment which seeks to serve the domestic market is at least as important as export-oriented foreign investment.

We turn now to an examination of foreign trade policy and industrialization in an atmosphere of experimentation and innovation in the workers' self-management system of Yugoslavia. While both import and export policies will be examined, major emphasis will be on manufactured export expansion and industrialization. First, however, some historical perspective is provided in the next chapter.

---

[1] It should also be stressed that both policies can be misapplied. See Bhagwati, Krueger [1973, p. 420].

Chapter II: Historical Background

1. The Inter-War Period

The state of Yugoslavia officially came into being in 1918[1]. It had a population of 12.1 million in 1921, which had grown to 15.6 million in 1939[2]. The growth in production that took place prior to World War II was slow-paced, as the data in Table 1 indicate. The growth of GNP at 2.6 percent per annum together with the population growth rate of 1.5 percent imply that per capita product increased at about 1.1 percent per annum during the period.

Table 1 - Some Selected Economic Indices and Growth Rates - Pre-War Yugoslavia (1923 = 100)

	Index	Annual compound growth rate (percent)
	1939	1939/23
Gross national product	150	2.6
Industry	180	3.8
Agriculture	145	2.4
Exports[a]	85	-1.0
Imports[a]	88	-.8
Population	126	1.5

[a] 1925 = 100.

Source: Rows 1-3: Vratusa [1971, p. 149]. - Rows 4-5: Pertot [1970, pp. 10 sq.]. - Row 6: SZzS [Statistički godišnjak FNRJ 1958, p. 75].

Economic policies of the government included some assistance to agriculture. A land reform program was begun in 1919; agricultural exports were promoted via trade agreements in the 1930s. Industrial

[1] Prior to 1929 it was called the Kingdom of Serbs, Croats and Slovenes.
[2] SZzS [Statistički godišnjak SFRJ 1971, p. 74].

policy existed in the form of state enterprise (in iron and steel, salt, tobacco, oil refining and mining, among others), tax and transportation policies designed to aid industry, and incentives for foreign investment in the economy[1]. Import substitution was encouraged by one of the most protective tariff systems in Europe. Although state enterprise existed, the role played by private capital in the industry and mining sectors was not minor. Engineering, chemicals and petroleum refining were about 80 percent foreign controlled, while the mining of non-ferrous metals was under virtually complete foreign control [Neuberger 1957, p. 199]. Economic policy pertaining to the public sector was highly centralized in contrast to policies affecting the private sector. Outside the public sector a laissez-faire policy existed [ibid.]. Despite the industrialization policies of the government, only gradual growth and industrialization were achieved. Shortages of capital, skilled labor and management have been cited as crucial factors limiting economic progress [Tomasevich 1949, pp. 200 sq.]. Low growth has also been attributed to an underdeveloped capital goods sector and an over-emphasis on the production of consumer goods [Avsenek 1957, pp. 282-285].

The sectoral composition of the national income between 1923 and 1938 underwent moderate change (Table 2). As implied by the data in Table 1, the share of industry in the national income edged upward at a slow pace - at a rate of about one-fourth of one percent per year[2]. However, the share of industry in Yugoslav national income in 1938 compares favorably with that of other countries at the time. Table 3 contains data on the industrial and agri-

Table 2 - Structure of National Income, 1923, 1938 (percent)

Sector	1923	1938
Industry	20.6	24.6
Agriculture	51.5	50.3
Others	27.9	25.1

Source: 1923: Hoffman, Neal [1962, p. 300]. - Ekonomski Institut FNRJ [Privreda 1952, p. 170].

[1] This section on the economics of pre-war Yugoslavia is meant to be only a brief survey. For more on the inter-war Yugoslav economy, see Kerner (Ed.) [1949]. - Byrnes (Ed.) [1957]. - Bombelles [1968].

[2] Unless specified otherwise, references to the industrial sector will be taken to mean manufacturing, mining and energy production.

cultural shares of 11 other countries[1]. As can be seen, the Yugoslav manufacturing and mining share exceeded the 12-country average and was about 39 percent greater than the average of the 5 currently

Table 3 - Gross Domestic Product per Capita and Sectoral Origin of Net Domestic Product at Factor Cost, 1937, 1938

Country	Gross domestic product per capita	Manufacturing and mining	Agriculture
	1937	1938[a]	
	US $ of 1955	percent	
Argentina	510	17	24
Denmark	840	18	25
Germany	685	44	13
Italy	260	26	27
Japan	185	32	20
Mexico	230	22	20
Netherlands	600	24	7
Norway	790	25	14
Puerto Rico	240	12	31
Turkey	200	12	47
United States	1,330	24	9
Yugoslavia[b]	175	25	50
Average:			
All countries		23	24
Seven currently MDCs		28	16
Five currently LDCs		18	34

[a]Germany, 1936, and Puerto Rico, 1939. - [b]Share in national income.

Source: Sectoral origin from UN [Statistical Yearbook 1956, pp. 473-476]. - GDP per capita from Maizels [1970, Table B2].

[1] The choice of countries in this table was influenced by data availability and a desire for diversified coverage.

less developed or semi-industrialized countries in the table. The share of the Yugoslav agricultural sector was the largest of this group of countries. The non-industrial, non-agricultural sectors taken as a group were therefore relatively underdeveloped. Since the industrial and agricultural shares did not undergo pronounced change during the inter-war period, it would appear that these sectors were relatively large upon the inception of the state[1].

The share of the labor force employed in agriculture and forestry was slightly higher and the share in industry slightly lower in 1938 than in 1931 (Table 4). The increase in the share of the labor force employed in agriculture and forestry provides indication of a lack of

Table 4 - Occupational Structure of the Employed Labor Force, 1931, 1938 (percent)

Sector	1931	1938
Agriculture and forestry	76.3	77.8
Mining and manufacturing	4.3	3.8
Handicrafts	6.5	4.9
Transport	1.3	1.2
Commerce and tourism	2.8	2.4
Administration, social services and others	8.8	9.9

Source: Hamilton [1968, p. 118].

employment opportunities in other sectors of the economy. This is further borne out by the decrease in the employment shares of handicrafts, and commerce and tourism, in addition to industry, and the constant share of transport. The relative increase in employment in administration, social services and others, that is, in the bureaucratic area, despite a falling share of national income experienced by this sector, is indicative of the existence of disguised unemployment. Total industrial employment approximately doubled during the period between the wars, reaching a level of about 300,000 in 1938. Meanwhile population was increasing by about 3.5 million. Assuming

[1] Of the combined industry and mining output in 1938, mining accounted for 8 percent and the food and textile industries 38.3 percent of the total [Bombelles 1968, p. 5].

a labor force participation rate of this population increment of 50 percent, the labor force increased by about 1.75 million, of which only approximately 8 percent was absorbed by the industrial sector.

Yugoslav exports prior to World War II consisted predominantly of raw materials and semi-processed goods. The leading export was timber, which accounted for 15-20 percent of total exports. Major import items included iron and steel products, raw cotton and cotton yarn and products (a more detailed breakdown of the inter-war foreign trade structure can be found in Tables A1 and A2 in the Statistical Appendix).

Manufactured exports accounted for about 14 percent of total exports during 1925-1930 and slightly less than 20 percent during 1931-1939. The share of manufactured imports, while experiencing a slight decline, averaged about 75 percent of total imports [Pertot 1958, pp. 14 sq.]. Imports of machinery, machine tools, electrotechnical products and transportation equipment ranged from 16 percent of total imports during 1921-1925 to 27 percent during 1936-1939. This trend would seem to indicate that the pace of industrialization quickened in the latter interwar years [Tomasevich 1949, p. 179]. A major change in the geographical orientation of exports and imports during the period was an increasing dependence on Germany. The share of total exports going to Germany almost tripled, reaching an average of 28.3 percent during 1936-1939. The share of imports from Germany more than doubled, being an average of 34.8 percent during 1936-1939 [Vucinich 1969, p. 36]. The Yugoslavian share of total world trade held at .4 to .5 percent during the 1930s [Tomasevich 1949, p. 174]. It is not surprising to find a lack of growth of trade during the 1930s, given the beggar-thy-neighbor policies at that time (see Table A3 for the index of export and import volume, 1925-1939). Another explanatory factor, especially with respect to import growth, is the suspension of German reparations payments which occured in 1931. These payments were equal to about 15 percent of Yugoslavia's total tax receipts between 1919 and 1931 [Vucinich 1969, p. 35].

The structure of Yugoslav exports and imports in 1939 was not untypical for a country at such a stage of development. Exports consisted primarily of raw materials and semi-manufactures; exports of capital goods and finished manufactures were, not surprisingly, a minor share of total exports. On the other hand, over 50 percent of imports consisted of finished goods; similarly capital and consumer goods represented over one-half of imports (Table 5). In every year from 1931 to 1939 the trade balance was positive, in contrast to a persistent deficit in the post-war period.

Table 5 - Structure of Exports and Imports by Stage of Production and Use of Products, 1939 (percent)

Stage of production	Exports	Imports	Use of products	Exports	Imports
Raw materials	55	20	Raw materials and semi-manufactures	78	49
Semi-finished goods	39	26	Capital goods	0	28
Finished goods	6	54	Consumer goods	22	33

Source: SZzS [Jugoslavija 1945-1964, p. 207].

On the eve of World War II Yugoslavia was a poor country. About three-fourths of the population made its living from agriculture. Exports in the main consisted of primary products and industrial raw materials. The industrial sector accounted for about one-quarter of the national income. Slovenia, Vojvodina, Croatia and Serbia (mainly because of Belgrade) were at higher stages of industrialization than the other republics and autonomous areas (Table 6). The Yugoslav

Table 6 - Occupational Structure of the Population by Republic and Autonomous Areas, 1939 (percent)

Area	Industry	Services	Other
Slovenia	18	17	65
Croatia	10	13	76
Vojvodina	13	11	76
Serbia (excluding Belgrade)	7	6	87
Serbia (including Belgrade)	18	13	69
Kosovo-Metchija	6	4	90
Bosnia-Herzegovina	6	8	86
Macedonia	6	9	85
Montenegro	6	11	83

Source: Hamilton [1968, p. 132].

per capita income in 1937 of 175 US $ of 1955 is the lowest of the small, geographically wide-ranging sample of countries in Table 3[1].

2. Central Planning 1946-1952

The Yugoslav economic plant was severely damaged during World War II. Close to 40 percent of the manufacturing industry was destroyed or badly damaged [Horvat 1971, p. 71]. Human loss was also great; about 11 percent of the population was killed during the war and 25 percent was left without shelter, 50 percent of the livestock and agricultural equipment was destroyed as well as the same share of the railways and rolling stock [Dirlam, Plummer 1973, p. 15].

The coming to power of the Communist Party under Josip Broz Tito brought with it radical changes in the economic system. Most of the non-agricultural sector of the economy was nationalized in 1946. The Federal Planning Commission was established in May of that year. The economic policy of central planning, administrative socialism, or étatism, as it has variously been called, was born. It was to succumb by 1952. The Yugoslavs copied the Soviet economic system more closely than any other eastern European country. Economic policy was oriented toward development via industrialization[2]. Within the industrial sector, heavy industry received major emphasis; self-sufficiency in capital goods was a high-priority goal.

The First Five-Year Plan appeared in the spring of 1947 and covered the period 1947-1951. In addition to the Five-Year Plan, there were annual, quarterly and ten-day plans[3]. The plan set very high goals

---

[1] The countries in Table 3 are not meant to constitute a representative sample. No African countries are included and the Asian and Latin American countries are among the richest of those continents.

[2] The economic policy orientation at this time is aptly described in the following statement by Boris Kidrič, who was President of the Economic Council of the Government and Chairman of the Federal Planning Commission at the time of the First Five-Year Plan: "The basic objective condition for further successes in socio-economic development which began in our country, is the industrialization of our country. The one who does not grasp this will understand nothing in our economic as well as social evolution. Consequently, in the near future all of our economic policy must be dedicated to the industrialization of our country." [Kidrič 1946, p. 16, quoted in Mišić 1965, p. 9].

[3] The weight of the annual plan, 3,300 pounds, provides an idea of the degree of planning.

for the economy. National income was to increase by a factor of 1.9, agricultural output by 1.5, and industrial output by 4.9 (all compared to the levels of 1939). Foreign trade came under complete control of the state. Imports were viewed as a necessity for the fulfillment of the plan; exports were a means of disposing of surplus production. Certain events occurred that helped to prevent the goals of the plan from being realized[1]. These included an economic blockade by the Cominform countries, drought, and collectivization efforts in agriculture[2]. Disillusionment with administrative socialism developed; the system of central planning broke down. This imitative phase of post-war Yugoslav economic policy was to be replaced by a policy of innovation. It is this dynamic system which is the subject of the following chapters.

---

[1] The index of agricultural production (1930-1939 average = 100) stood at 89 in 1947 and 75 in 1952 [Yugoslav Survey, Vol. 11, 1970, No. 4, p. 4]. - The index of industrial production (1939 = 100) was at a level of 121 in 1947 and 166 in 1952 [SZzS, Industrija 1973, p. 11].

[2] See Bombelles [1968, pp. 45 sq.] for an argument that the economic blockade was not the decisive factor in the failure of the economy to reach its planned growth. A different view is taken by George Macesich [1969, p. 208].

Chapter III: Economic Policy and Institutional Change under the Workers' Self-Management System, with Special Reference to Foreign Trade and Payments Policy

1. Economic Policy and Institutional Change - General

a. The Inaugural Stage - 1952-1961

In this chapter we shall begin with some remarks about economic policy in general since the introduction of the workers' self-management system. Then follows an examination in some detail of foreign trade and payments policies.

A new economic system began to evolve in 1950 with the establishment of workers' councils in many enterprises. Following a transitional period of legal activity and institutional adaptation, the new system of workers' self-management became operational by 1952. The former state enterprises became socially owned property administered by working collectives. The autonomy of the enterprise was severely limited, however. For example, the enterprise had little room to manoeuvre in matters concerning the distribution of its net income (gross income less material costs). The local commune had an especially strong voice in enterprise operations. Detailed central planning, in which individual enterprises received output quotas, was replaced by a system of planning by basic proportions. Enterprises had to follow certain rules, such as minimum capacity utilization, but they no longer had specific output quotas to meet. The federal economic plan determined certain basic proportions, such as consumption, the rate of accumulation and the distribution of investment[1]. Since the beginning of Yugoslavia's particular brand of socialism, a continuous process of change and adaptation has been experienced.

---

[1] Some degree of caution should be exercised in estimating the magnitude of change associated with the new economic system. After noting the increased importance of monetary and fiscal policy, the abolishment of controls on the physical output of enterprises, and the increased role played by banks in the investment process, Bombelles adds: "The planning process was not decentralized; top political leadership still made basic economic decisions ... the same people having the same objectives and using basically the same strategies, continued to develop Yugoslavia" [Bombelles 1968, p. 71]. The investment process was not decentralized until the mid-1960s.

Emphasis on the construction of large-scale industrial projects and basic infrastructure begun during the period of central planning was continued into the beginning of what we have termed the inaugural stage of the workers' self-management system. Heavy industry was given priority over light industry; within heavy industry the production of machinery and equipment was stressed[1]. In other words, industrialization strategy remained largely as it was as key projects were being completed. Profitability or competitiveness of production were not important decision variables in the building of industries.

The abandonment of administrative socialism carried with it an end to the state foreign trade monopoly. A step in the direction of a more liberalized foreign trade and payments system was taken in 1952. The exchange rate, which previously was without economic meaning, was changed from 50 to 300 dinars per U.S. dollar. At the same time a system of export and import coefficients was introduced. These coefficients were multiplied by the official exchange rate (and later by the settlement rate) to determine the receipts and payments in dinars of exporters and importers. The system of multiple exchange rates remained in force, with revisions, until 1961. Foreign trade liberalization was to prove very difficult to achieve; reforms in the external sector lagged behind those in other areas.

In the mid-1950s there was a shift in industrialization policy. Light industry received greater emphasis and heavy industry, especially ferrous metallurgy, less. There was also a reduction of the share of industry in total gross fixed investment. Whereas in 1952-1956, 52.5 percent of gross fixed investment was in industry, the share in 1956-1961 was 35.8 percent. Heavy industry received 86 percent of industrial investment in 1952-1956 and 72 percent in 1956-1961. The share of ferrous metallurgy fell from 16.2 to 5.5 percent (Table 7). This shift in policy toward a more even development of the industrial sector can be attributed to a reaction to uprisings in Poland and Hungary caused by shortages of consumer goods, improvement in the climate of foreign affairs (relations with eastern Europe improved), accomplishments in building up the economic infrastructure, and the

---

[1] Included in the definition of heavy industry are mineral extraction, energy, metallurgy, chemicals, building materials, non-metallic mineral industries, metalworking, mechanical and electrical engineering. The category of light industry includes food processing, textiles, leather, paper, wood products and printing. The Yugoslav industrial classification is similar to, but not identical with, the Standard Industrial Classification.

Table 7 - Structure of Yugoslav Industrial Investment, 1947-1972 (percent)[a]

Industry branch	1947-1951	1952-1956	1956-1961	1961-1965	1965-1972	1952-1972
Electrical energy	17.8	23.3	22.8	19.9	23.7	22.5
Coal and coke	11.5	8.1	9.3	5.4	4.5	6.5
Crude petroleum	4.5	3.5	2.1	3.8	3.3	3.5
Ferrous metals	11.6	16.2	5.5	10.5	12.5	11.2
Non-ferrous metals	9.7	8.4	6.8	5.2	8.9	7.7
Non-metallic minerals	5.2	6.1	3.0	2.5	2.3	3.3
Metal products	10.1	6.5	6.4	9.8	7.9	8.0
Shipbuilding	.3	.6	.9	.9	1.0	.9
Electrical machinery, etc.	3.0	2.4	1.7	3.0	3.0	2.6
Chemicals	3.2	6.8	6.8	8.8	7.4	7.3
Building materials	3.0	1.0	2.7	2.7	3.5	2.7
Wood products	7.0	3.2	3.7	3.7	3.4	3.5
Paper and paper products	1.2	2.6	3.3	5.2	2.4	3.2
Textiles	4.4	3.9	6.3	7.3	5.2	5.6
Leather and footwear	.8	.5	1.1	.9	.9	.9
Rubber	.4	.3	.6	.9	.7	.6
Food products	5.0	4.8	8.4	5.3	5.4	5.9
Printing and publishing	.2	.6	1.1	1.3	1.6	1.2
Tobacco manufactures	.4	.5	.8	.6	.7	.7
Motion pictures	.4	.1	.2	.1	.1	.1
Mining explorations	-	-	.4	1.3	.4	.4
Miscellaneous manufactures	.2	1.0	3.6	1.0	1.2	1.6

[a]Totals do not always add up to 100, owing to rounding.

Source: Institut za ekonomisku investicija [Investicije 1947-1969, pp. 13, 93-178]. - SZzS [Industrijska preduzeća 1968, p. 30; 1970, p. 33]. - SZzS [Statistički godišnjak SFRJ 1974, p. 289].

difficulty of financing the development of heavy industry. Part of the strategy was to tax industries which were in a position to accumulate income rapidly.

b. The Reform Stage - 1961-...

The period beginning with 1961 and extending to the present we have called the reform stage of development. It includes the major economic reforms of 1961 and 1965[1]. These reforms came on the heels of a very successful completion of the Five-Year Plan of 1957-1961. The plan was declared fulfilled after four years. On the domestic scene, the 1961 reforms were directed mainly toward the banking, financial and income distribution systems. The proportion of the earnings of enterprises put at their own disposal was increased[2]. Flat-rate taxes replaced progressive taxes on enterprise income. The banking system was decentralized. Short-term lending was transferred from the National Bank (the Yugoslav central bank) to communal banks; republic banks were set up and political control of banking operations was relaxed. The 1961 reforms were in the main aimed at expanding the role of the market and increasing the country's international competitiveness.

The dinar was devalued in 1961 and the multiple exchange rate system ostensibly abandoned. The system of export and import coefficients was replaced by an import tariff and export subsidy arrangement. Exports were mainly free of control, although certain goods, chiefly primary products, were subject to quota or permit. Export proceeds had to be surrendered to the National Bank; part of the proceeds, 7 percent for most industrial exports, could be repurchased by the enterprises. About 20 percent of imports were liberalized, others were subject to permit or quota.

The first two years into the 1960s were problem years for the Yugoslav economy. Inflation, relatively slow growth and an aggravating balance-of-payments deficit were the major sore spots. The Five-Year Plan of 1961-1965 was abandoned. A vigorous debate ensued between supporters of further decentralization and reliance on the market and advocates of a shift toward more centralization. The views of the former prevailed. The decision to decentralize further and

---

[1] The reform of 1965 was of considerably greater scope than the 1961 reform. However, significant reform of the foreign trade and payments system took place in 1961. Thus 1961 was chosen as the dividing point between the inaugural and reform stage of development under the workers' self-management system.

[2] The proportion of the social product, that is, value-added, of the enterprises at their own disposal (i.e., net personal income, enterprise funds and depreciation) was 42.8 percent in 1959 and 50 percent in 1961. [Yugoslav Survey, Vol. 11, 1970, No. 3, p. 82].

strengthen the role of the market was made official when the federal parliament in 1965 put its approval on the next reform. The reform had both short-term and long-term objectives. Short-run goals included an easing of inflation, moving the balance of payments toward equilibrium, reducing unemployment and increasing industrial capacity utilization. Longer-term objectives were concerned with increasing economic efficiency by relying more on the market mechanism. The price system was to be reformed, growth and investment policies revised, foreign trade liberalized and international competitiveness improved [Bićanić 1972, p. 233].

The economic reform of 1965 was somewhat similar to the one of 1961, although in 1965 there was to be a stronger drive toward decentralization and becoming more internationally competitive. The dinar was devalued and tariffs and import controls reduced. The price system was restructured so as to bring prices more in line with world prices and to correct distortions in relative prices. Since the new price policy was likely to stimulate inflation, price controls were extended to 90 percent of the products[1]. Additional steps were taken in 1965 to increase the share of enterprise net income not subject to external control. This share, defined as the sum of net personal incomes, depreciation and enterprise funds, increased from 54 percent in 1964 to 59 percent in 1965. The 1965 reform shifted the source of investment funds to the banks and enterprises and away from the government[2]. Direct taxes on enterprises were eliminated and the incidence of the turnover tax was shifted from wholesale to retail enterprises [Crawford 1970, p. 612]. Greater funds would thus be available for reinvestment by the enterprises. Responsibility for transmitting so-called contributions on personal incomes remained with the enterprise[3].

Since the creation in 1955 of the Federal Price Office, a system of administratively controlled prices has evolved. Certain goods have been subject to fixed prices, others to ceiling prices, control on the basis of advance approval, and minimum prices. Price freezes have also been applied from time to time. The price reforms of 1961 and 1965 both had the purpose of reducing price distortions by increasing agricultural and raw material prices relative to the prices of manu-

[1] OECD [Economic Survey 1966, p. 8]. - Price controls were subsequently relaxed. The proportion of industrial products covered by price controls was 48 percent in 1968 [ibid., 1970, p. 14].

[2] See section 3 of this chapter.

[3] For additional information on the tax system see Dirlam, Plummer [1973, pp. 186-193].

factured goods. Previously the prices of primary products had been kept artificially low in relation to prices of manufactured goods; this price policy was designed to further industrialization[1]. Producers' prices of industrial goods rose by 4 percent in 1961, agricultural goods prices by 15 percent and retail prices by 8 percent (Table A 4). In 1965 industrial producers' prices increased by 15 percent, agricultural producers' prices by 43 percent and retail prices by 29 percent; the rate of inflation as shown by the implicit social product deflator was 28.4 percent. The ratio of the index of prices of manufactured goods to that of agricultural goods reveals that the terms of trade for agricultural goods have been increasing during the entire 1952-1972 period. After a period of gradual improvement, the rate of increase picked up during the first half of the 1960s, reflecting the price reforms referred to above. The agricultural terms of trade have continued to improve.

2. The Evolution of Foreign Trade and Payments Policy

a. Foreign Trade and Payments Policy, 1952-1960

As noted previously, the abandonment of the system of central planning meant the end of the state foreign trade monopoly. As early as 1949 there were 119 organizations registered for foreign trade operations. These were predominantly specialized agencies under the control of the Ministry of Foreign Trade. Today, as long as certain minimum standards are met, e.g., adequate trained personnel and minimum fixed asset value, productive enterprises are free to engage in foreign trade operations.

The previously meaningless foreign exchange rate of 50 dinars per U.S. dollar was replaced in December 1951 with a rate of 300 dinars = \$ 1 (Table 8). At the same time a system of export and import coefficients was introduced. Under this multiple exchange rate system, the official (and beginning in 1954 the settlement rate of 632 dinars = \$ 1) exchange rate was multiplied by the appropriate coefficient to yield the effective exchange rate. The coefficients varied according to commodity. The export coefficients ranged between .5 and 6 during 1952-1960; during any one time the number of coefficients ranged

[1] This policy contributed to bottlenecks in the supply of primary inputs and also tended to raise the imported input component of production (see Chapter V).

Table 8 - Yugoslav Exchange Rates, 1952-1972 (dinars per US $)

Year	Official rate	Export rate[e]	Import rate[f]	Emigrant rate[g]	Free market rate[h]	Black market rate[i]	Settlement rate[j]	Tourist and diplomat rate[k]
1952	300[a]	240 -1,800	240 -3,000		647	425 - 725		
1953		240 -1,800	240 -3,000		1,910	450 - 600		
1954		316 -2,528	316 -2,528	600	379	525 - 710	632	
1955		316 -1,896	316 -2,528		940	725 - 850		
1956		316 -1,896	316 -1,896		5,020	835 - 925		400
1957		316 -1,264	379.20-1,896		6,909	710 - 825		
1958		379.20-1,264	632 -1,896		8,217	750 - 815		
1959		505.60-1,264	632 -1,580		9,725	725 - 817		
1960		505.60-1,264	632 -1,580			745 -1,000	632	400
1961				600		765 -1,005	750	600
1962						800 - 928		
1963						802 - 945		
1964	300					865 -1,059		
1965	1,250[b]					980 -1,570	750	
1966	12.50					13.50- 16.00		
1967						12.75- 14.50		
1968						12.65- 14.10		
1969						12.50- 14.15		
1970	12.50					12.95- 15.00		
1971	15.00[c]					15.45- 17.95		
1972	17.00[d]							

[a]As of December 28, 1951 when it was changed from Din 50 per U.S. dollar. The official rate had virtually no operational significance in the 1955-1964 period. - [b]As of July 26, 1965. On January 1, 1966 a new dinar equal to 100 old dinars was introduced. - [c]This rate became effective on January 22, 1971. - [d]Became effective on December 21, 1971. - [e]These are the rates applicable to sales of foreign exchange by exporting enterprises. They are derived by applying various coefficients to the settlement rate of exchange (to the official rate prior to 1954). The coefficient varied with respect to commodities. Between 1952 and 1960 the coefficient ranged between .5 and 6 and the number of coefficients ranged from 12 to 35 at any one time. - [f]These are the rates applicable to purchases of foreign exchange by Yugoslav importing enterprises. They are derived in the same way as the export rates. Between 1952 and 1960 import coefficients ranged between .5 and 10.0. Lower coefficients were applied to foreign exchange purchased to import "essential" goods with higher coefficients for "less essentials" and luxuries. The system of export and import coefficients was replaced by an import tariff and export subsidy system in 1961. - [g]Applicable to receipts from emigrants' remittances and certain other non-commercial items. Discontinued after 1961. - [h]End-of-year rates. As of 1956 the free market was taken over by the National Bank where it sold exchange for a few imports and invisibles (less than 1 percent of total sales of foreign exchange). Previously exporters could sell exchange that was part of their retention quota in the free market. Terminated after 1959. - [i]Extremes of end-of-month rates on U.S. banknotes and/or unlicensed transfers to New York. - [j]The rate applicable to most commercial transactions (after being multiplied by the appropriate export or import coefficient) from December 1954 to July 1965 (became unified settlement rate as of January 15, 1961). - [k]Rate for foreign tourists and diplomats in Yugoslavia. Discontinued after 1961.

Source: IMF [various issues]. - Pick's Currency Yearbook [various issues].

between 12 and 35. Import coefficients varied between .5 and 10 during the same period.

The number and magnitude of these coefficients underwent frequent change. They were supposedly designed to further the goal of rapid industrialization with concentration on the development of heavy industry. Thus the export coefficients were kept high for manufactured exports, especially for such key products as ferrous and non-ferrous metals. Import coefficients for raw materials, semi-manufactures and capital goods were maintained at a low level relative to those for consumer goods. Thus in 1957 the effective exchange rate for industrial exports was 1,059 dinars = $ 1, while the rate for exports of agricultural goods was 655 dinars (Table 9). The effective exchange

Table 9 - Effective Exchange Rates, 1957

Exports	Effective exchange rate	Subsidy[a]	Imports	Effective exchange rate	Subsidy[a]
	dinars per US $	percent		dinars per US $	percent
Industry	1,059	35	Raw materials and semi-manufactures	766	2
Agriculture	655	-16	Consumer goods	1,612	-105
Forestry	675	-10	Food	568	29
Services	620	-21	Capital goods	617	21
All	858	10	Services	508	35
			All	719	9

Average effective rate: 789

[a]Subsidy defined as difference between exports (imports) valued at effective and average effective exchange rates (789 dinars = $ 1). This difference was then taken as a percentage of exports (imports) valued at the average effective rate.

Source: Frković [1957, p. 86].

rate for imports of raw materials and semi-manufactures was 766 and that of capital goods 617 dinars. A feature of the system was that industrial enterprises found it easier to push for a change in the exchange rate coefficient, e.g., an increase in the export coefficient, rather than attempt to increase the efficiency of production. Quantitative import restrictions were also a part of the system.

A free foreign exchange market was established in 1951 where exporters could sell a portion of their foreign exchange earnings. The foreign exchange retention quota initially ranged between 20 and 45 percent. By 1956 the retention quota had been reduced to one percent and the free market was taken over by the National Bank. It was discontinued altogether in 1960.

b. Foreign Trade and Payments Policy, 1961-1965

Major changes in the foreign trade and payments system took place in 1961. Aims of the reforms included liberalization of the foreign trade system and greater participation in the international economy. The dinar was devalued from 632 to 750 dinars per U.S. dollar. The system of export and import coefficients was replaced by a system of tariffs, import quotas and licences, foreign exchange retention quotas, export premiums and subsidies, and limited export restrictions. "Temporary" export premiums were to serve as a means of easing the strain associated with the termination of export coefficients and to favor certain industries thought to be potentially competitive but as yet unable to compete unaided in world markets. Export premiums applied to about one-half of total exports and consisted of three categories in which the export value was increased by 10, 22 or 32 percent. Export premiums and subsidies reached about 300 billion (old) dinars in 1964, which amounted to about 45 percent of the value of exports.

In spite of the rather heavy subsidization of exports, enterprises experienced difficulty adapting to the discontinuance of exchange rate coefficients; the growth rate of exports declined from 19 percent in 1960 to less than one-half of one percent in 1961 (the growth rate rebounded to 21 percent in 1962). The foreign exchange retention quota, which enterprises could use largely at their own discretion, varied from 3 percent of export earnings for agricultural exports to 7 percent for services and industrial products and 25 percent for printing and publishing exports[1].

---

[1] For more detailed information on the foreign trade and payments reforms of 1961 see OECD [Economic Survey 1962, 1963]. - Yugoslav Sur-

The nominal devaluation of the dinar from 632 to 750 dinars = $ 1 overstates the real devaluation in terms of the effective export foreign exchange rate. The effective export exchange rate (taking export premiums and subsidies into account) in 1960 had reached 981 dinars per U.S. dollar in comparison to the nominal exchange rate of 632 dinars per dollar. In 1961 the effective export exchange rate was 1,021 dinars per dollar. Thus the devaluation in terms of the effective export exchange rate was 3.9 percent, while the nominal devaluation was 15.7 percent[1]. The effective export exchange rate increased slightly to 1,055 dinars = $ 1 in 1964. Manufactured exports were favored with the highest dinar/dollar rate (Table 10). Shipbuilding, paper products, textiles (including clothing) and metal products received the most favorable exchange rates among the manufactured exports.

Turning briefly to import policy, a tariff system was introduced in 1961 as part of Yugoslavia's move toward full membership in the GATT[2]. Tariff rates ranged up to 60 percent, with the higher rates applying to consumer goods. The average rate for capital goods was 34 percent and for semi-finished goods and raw materials 10 percent. The average tariff rate in 1962 was 18.8 percent[3]. There was also an import licence and quota system. About one-fourth of imports could be freely imported, while another one-fifth could be imported on the basis of a general licence. The amount of imports permitted under the general licence scheme was related to the enterprise's imports in the previous year, e.g., in 1961 foreign exchange amounting to 80 percent of that used in 1960 was permitted. Imports of capital goods, amounting to 20-25 percent of total imports, were controlled by the Yugoslav Investment Bank, providing the bank with an instrument for regulating the amount and form of investment.

---

vey [1961, pp. 673-680; 1963, pp. 2029-2050]. - Bićanić [1973]. - Horvat [1971]. - A special retention quota of 10 percent for machinery exports and 12 percent for exports of motor vehicles and tractors was established in 1963.

[1] Horvat [1971, p. 126]. - As Kovač [1973] has pointed out, the seemingly sharp devaluations of the dinar are somewhat deceiving. Devaluations tended to occur when the official exchange rate deviated from the effective rate to such an extent that difficulties in maintaining the difference became too great. Consequently the exchange rate policy in practice led to an exchange rate that could better be described as fluctuating rather than fixed.

[2] Yugoslavia became a full member of GATT in 1966 after becoming an associate member in 1959 and a provisional member in 1962.

[3] The average tariff rate rose to 23.3 percent in 1964; the average rate on manufactured imports was 26.4 and on capital goods 42.0 percent.

Table 10 - Effective Exchange Rates, 1963, 1964

Industrial branch	Effective export exchange rates	
	1963	1964
	dinars per US $	
Coal	1, 114	1, 104
Crude petroleum	1, 035	1, 110
Ferrous metals	1, 104	1, 080
Non-ferrous metals	1, 002	984
Non-metallic minerals	1, 050	1, 014
Metal products	1, 137	1, 158
Shipbuilding	1, 212	1, 212
Electrical machinery, etc.	1, 089	1, 101
Chemicals	1, 116	1, 050
Building materials	1, 068	1, 014
Wood products	993	1, 056
Paper, etc.	1, 113	1, 164
Textiles	1, 146	1, 163
Leather	1, 008	990
Rubber products	930	1, 065
Food products	984	993

	1964 effective exchange rates	
	import	export
	dinars per US $	
Total industry		1, 114
Agriculture		918
Forestry		860
Transport		1, 001
Tourism		915
Average	925	1, 055
Range	810-1, 050	750-1, 300
Raw materials	810	
Semi-manufactures	862	
Consumer goods	1, 050	
Capital goods	1, 028	

Dinars per US $	Structure of 1964 effective export exchange rates	
	total exports	industrial exports
	percent	
750	2. 7	1. 4
751- 900	5. 9	5. 4
901-1, 000	29. 2	15. 3
1, 001-1, 100	29. 4	27. 6
1, 101-1, 200	19. 1	28. 2
1, 201-1, 260	11. 2	17. 9
above 1, 260	2. 5	4. 2

Source: Džeba, Beslać [1965, pp. 76 sq.].

The liberalizing aims of the reforms were not achieved. By 1965, import restrictions and export subsidies had expanded as the nation retreated somewhat from its advance toward freer trade. Multiple exchange rates in effect had reappeared, albeit in a different form, and tariff rates had moved upward.

c. Foreign Trade and Payments Policy since 1965[1]

The next major external sector reforms took place during 1965-1967. Greater integration into the world economy consistent with the nation's comparative advantage was to be achieved by vigorous efforts to liberalize foreign trade and by improvements in efficiency resulting from pursuing a more intensive growth strategy. Exports were to expand more rapidly than imports, and a balance-of-payments surplus and convertibility of the dinar were to be realized eventually.

The dinar was devalued in July 1965 to 1,250 dinars per U.S. dollar (with the currency reform of January 1966 in which 100 old dinars were made equal to one new dinar, the exchange rate became 12.5 new dinars = $ 1). Export subsidies were, with one or two exceptions, abolished (but as in the previous reform, were soon reintroduced). Foreign exchange retention quotas remained as the major export promotion tool. The retention quota was 7 percent in most cases; the quota was 10 percent for exports of selected capital goods and pharmaceuticals, 12 percent for exports of road motor vehicles and tractors, and 20 percent for most service exports. These basic rates increased with the share of total sales exported to a maximum quota of twice the basic quota for export shares above 60 percent. This export stimulation device was strengthened in 1972 when the basic retention quota was increased from 7 to 20 percent. Quotas of 45 and 100 percent, respectively, became applicable to tourist services and Yugoslav enterprises operating abroad, e.g., construction and engineering firms.

Further devaluations of the dinar took place in 1971, when the official exchange rate became 15 dinars = $ 1 in January and 17 dinars = $ 1 in December. On a trade-weighted basis, the December devaluation was of the order of 20 percent [OECD, Economic Survey 1972, p. 22]. The dinar was again devalued in February 1973, along with the 10 percent devaluation of the dollar. A limited foreign exchange market was opened in mid-1973, followed closely by a decision to abandon fixed exchange rates. The float of the dinar is not a "clean" float, however,

[1] For further information on reforms since 1965, see OECD [Economic Survey 1965 ff.]. - Horvat [1971]. - Bićanić [1973]. - Milenkovitch [1971]. - Jančić [1967]. - Domandžić [1966].

since the National Bank provides a considerable amount of guidance for the dinar.

In mid-1971 a 6 percent ad valorem subsidy for exports to convertible currency areas and Poland was introduced. Exports have also been encouraged through export credit policy, which has become a major promotion tool. In 1972 the financing of exports was liberalized in a bid to stimulate exports. In a further effort to encourage exports, the repayment terms for credits to producers of export goods were extended from 18 months to two years in October 1974.

Another economic policy change that was at least partially export-motivated was the decision taken in 1967 to allow foreign direct investment in the form of joint ventures between Yugoslav and foreign firms. The less than enthusiastic response of foreign firms to the possibility of investing in Yugoslavia led in 1971 to a major liberalization of the regulations pertaining to such investment. One of the conditions required for approval of a joint venture is that a substantial share of the production be exported[1].

Import policy since 1965 has been subject to oscillations, becoming first less and then more restrictive. These shifts in policy can be at least partially traced to changes in policy emphasis between balance of payments and price considerations. A new tariff schedule was introduced in 1965. The average tariff rate was reduced from 23.29 percent in 1964 to 10.50 percent in 1965. The traditional cascading tariff pattern existed, as the average tariff rates on raw materials, semi-finished products, capital goods and consumer goods were 5, 9, 20, and 21 percent, respectively. About one-fourth of imports was liberalized in 1967, while a complicated system of restrictions applied to the rest, e.g., certain imports from the convertible currency area were made conditional upon the purchase of a specific quantity of clearing currency. This policy of tying imports from the convertible area to those from the clearing area was motivated by a desire to reduce surpluses in trade with the clearing area.

The average tariff level in 1971 was 12.1 percent (Table A 5). Although this level does not appear high by developing country standards, it understates the degree of protection accorded domestic producers. Customs and border taxes add another 4 percent to the import duties. Additionally, an import surcharge of up to 10 percent has been used since 1970. There is also at present a customs inspection tax of 1 percent and "tax equalization duty" of 5 percent. Moreover, the effective tariff generally exceeds the nominal tariff (Table A 6). And finally,

[1] Chapter VI deals with foreign direct investment.

import restrictions in the form of licences and quotas are probably more important protective devices than are tariffs. Import liberalization took place in 1972, following a tightening of import restrictions in 1970. Import policy became more liberal in the first half of 1974 but was followed by an opposite movement in the second half of the year. In 1974, 60 percent of imports were fully liberalized, 14 percent were liberalized subject to foreign exchange availability, and 26 percent were restricted. The shares of these three import categories in 1967 were 39, 56 and 5 percent, respectively. The overall trend of the past few years appears to be towards greater liberalization. A movement to reverse this trend is currently under way.

3. Indirect Export Promotion Policies

Exports may be fostered by economic policies other than those which are direct components of the system of foreign trade and payments. In fact most economic policies affect export possibilities in some way. A complete examination of all these policies is beyond the scope of this study. Investment and price policies, which have played strategic roles in the entire development strategy and have been instrumental in shaping the external sector, have been singled out for review because of their relevance to a discussion of export promotion measures[1].

Investment policy under the workers' self-management system was initially organized according to a system of social investment loan funds. These funds were established at the federal, republic, district and communal levels. Hundreds of these public investment funds existed. The major investment fund, however, was the General Investment Fund, which in 1958 handled 81 percent of the investment allocations. Sources of revenues accruing to the various investment funds consisted of a 6 percent tax on the fixed assets of enterprises (for the privilege of using social capital)[2], taxes and levies on enterprise income, and interest payments on credit and repayments of loans. The combination of extra-budgetary financing of these funds and an inten-

---

[1] This section relies on information contained in Bićanić [1973]. - UNCTAD [1964a]. - Horvat [1971]. - See Table 7 for information on the structure of industrial investment.

[2] This tax, or interest rate, on social capital was set at a lower rate for some industries, e.g., 4 percent for ferrous metallurgy, 2 percent for transportation and 1 percent for electrical power generation and coal production. The basic rate was lowered to 4 percent in 1965, along with a revaluation of enterprise fixed assets. The tax was discontinued in 1971.

sive desire on the part of the various governmental units to step up the tempo of development in their own areas produced such a demand for investment funds that the volume of investment during 1955-1960 exceeded that envisaged in the social plan by 20 percent.

Decisions on the allocation of investment funds on the macro level, i.e., sectoral allocations, were made by the economic plans. Micro-level decisions, i.e., the allocation of investment funds within economic sectors, were the province of specialized banks, e.g., the Yugoslav Investment Bank and the Foreign Trade Bank. These decisions regarding the allocation of funds between enterprises took the form of competitive bidding as well as direct contact. Among the stated criteria which were to be used in making decisions on the granting of investment loans were: export effect, import substitution effect, employment effect, interest rate, repayment period, gestation period, use of own resources and profitability. On paper these investment decision-making criteria look rather impressive. In practice, however, investment decisions were frequently based on political considerations; de facto control over investment rested with politicians. As each area wanted all the factories it could get, the outcome was uncoordinated investment decisions, unnecessary investment duplication and an uneconomic geographical pattern of investment.

In relating investment policy to the external sector it is important to examine the criteria used in evaluating the effect of an investment project on exports and imports, i.e., the foreign currency effect. The instrument used for measuring this effect was the ratio of the balance-of-payments effect (including exports generated and foregone and import requirements and substitutes) to the total investment in the project. While in Yugoslavia policies emphasizing import substitution have existed alongside those stressing export expansion, an interesting change in emphasis may be indicated by a 1963 regulation which authorized banks to extend credits only for export promoting purposes. This regulation superseded legislation which permitted the extension of credits for both export expansion and import substitution. Other projects could secure financing only through the directives of the Economic Development Plan. The 1963 Plan contained the provision that "... in channelling investment expenditure ... provisions should be made to secure priority to investments which are likely to increase our export possibilities, or assure the modernization and rationalization of production processes in export-oriented branches of industry" [UNCTAD 1964b, pp. 25, 31 sq.]. However, export planning in practice has been described as a process of intentionally building plants with excess capacity, with the hope that exports would arise as a "vent-for-surplus" [Dyker 1974, p. 338].

The economic reforms of the mid-1960s resulted in significant changes in investment policy. Consistent with the orientation of these reforms toward decentralization and greater reliance on the market mechanism, the social investment funds were abolished and business enterprises and banks became the major forces concerning investment decisions[1]. Taxes and levies on enterprises were reduced resulting in an increase in the share of enterprise net income which the firm could distribute according to its own decisions.

The main effect of the reforms on the source of finance of fixed investment was an increase in the rate of bank financing at the expense of the social investment funds. This is seen in Table 11 which shows that after a brief spurt the enterprise share returned to about what

Table 11 - Sources of Finance of Fixed Investment in the Social Sector, 1952-1972 (percent)

	1952	1953	1954	1955	1960	1962	1964	1966	1968	1970	1972
Social funds and budgets	98	87	74	64	52	59	36	16	16	16	19
Work organizations	2	13	26	35	37	38	32	46	37	33	38
Banks	-	-	-	1	1	3	32	39	47	51	43

Source: Horvat [1971, p. 140]. - SZzS [Statistički godišnjak SFRJ 1973, p. 213].

it was before the reform. While the decentralization of investment probably was motivated by both economic and political factors, the influence of potential borrowers and politicians on the banks' activities provides cause to wonder to what extent economic rationality became more important in the investment process. Steps were taken in 1972 to increase the influence of enterprises in the operations of banks, an indication perhaps that political considerations had continued to play a strong role in investment considerations[2]. The main impact

[1] Banks could be founded by enterprises and socio-political organizations. The direct participation of the latter in the establishment of banks has since been done away with.

[2] Bank lending policy is still biased as a result of the strong influence over such policy exerted by the founding members (enterprises) of the banks. The bias hinders the entry of new firms as existing enterprises do not look favorably upon additional competitors.

of these changes on foreign trade policies is that decisions pertaining to such issues as export promotion, import substitution and the structure of foreign trade have become more decentralized.

Yugoslav foreign trade policy can be characterized in terms of its willingness to change and adopt courses of action that at times represented more than marginal breaks from the past. The frequency and magnitude of institutional and policy change, in addition to the unique workers' self-management system, set Yugoslavia apart from most developing countries. Moreover, Yugoslavia does not conform to the common pattern of an extreme emphasis of policy on either import substitution or export promotion, with a sharp break in the direction of emphasis occuring at some point. Export promotion, in the form of exchange rate policy, export premiums and subsidies, and investment policy has been pursued along with an inward-oriented import policy.

As previously revealed, manufactured exports were favored with relatively high exchange rates during the period when multiple exchange rates existed. Exporters of manufactured goods benefited from subsidies, premiums, credit, taxation and foreign exchange disposal policies[1]. Furthermore, price policy in Yugoslavia has favored the production of manufactured goods relative to primary and semi-manufactured products. Prices of the latter goods were kept low in relation to the former in an attempt to encourage the growth of the manufacturing sector. This policy affected the competitiveness of manufactured exports, compounded the difficulty of evaluating comparative advantage and led to severe bottlenecks in the industrial sector at times and a greater reliance on imported inputs. A major attempt to correct the price distortions was made in the price reform of 1965. In addition to the rate of increase of agricultural prices that was three times greater than the increase of industrial prices (see section 1 of this chapter and Table A 4), within industry, prices of processing branches were to rise by 8 percent and raw material prices by 24 percent. Prices of iron ore, aluminium and crude steel were all to rise by over 40 percent; price decreases of 6, 9 and 10 percent were set for cotton fabrics, medicines and rubber footwear, respectively [Neuberger 1968, p. 373]. Finally, the legislation of 1967 allowing foreign direct investment in the form of joint ventures can be seen as an

[1] It has been suggested that the allocation of export aids was based more on what was needed to make the product competitive than on economic grounds (comment made by a Yugoslav economist in personal conversation); thus the less competitive industries received higher subsidies.

attempt to improve the manufactured export performance of the economy. The "Platform for the Preparation of Positions and Decisions of the Tenth Congress of the League of Communists of Yugoslavia" [Yugoslav Survey 1973] stressed the need for effective incorporation of the economy into the world division of labor and the importance of long-term forms of economic cooperation with other countries, e.g., production cooperation, specialization and joint ventures.

Chapter IV: Some Empirical Aspects of Industrialization under the Workers' Self-Management System

The strategy of economic development has stressed a high rate of investment together with strong emphasis on the growth of the industrial sector[1]. Economic growth during the past two decades has been rapid, albeit somewhat unstable. A bird's-eye view of the growth and structural change that has taken place is contained in Tables 12 and 13[2]. The growth of industrial exports and value-added (in constant prices) at 12.0 and 10.5 percent, respectively, has been particularly rapid. Industrial exports have climbed from 4.6 percent of industrial output in 1952 to 13.7 percent in 1973 (in current prices and exchange rates). The rise in the share of industry in the social product from 22.0 to 38.5 percent between 1952 and 1973 took place mainly at the expense of the agriculture and forestry sectors. Industrial growth, as well as the growth of total and per capita social product hold up well in an international comparison. The growth rate of Yugoslav industrial production exceeded that of the three country groups in Table 14; the growth of total output was greater than that experienced by the developing and developed market economy countries[3].

---

[1] The share of gross fixed capital formation in the social product (1966 prices) averaged 31 percent during 1952-1972.

[2] For a more detailed picture of quantitative economic development in Yugoslavia since 1952, see Dirlam, Plummer [1973]. - Bićanić [1973]. - World Bank [1975].

[3] The 1960-1970 growth rate calculated by the author from official Yugoslav data on net material product in 1966 prices is 6.5 percent. As previously noted, social product (SP), or gross material product, differs from GNP in that "non-productive" activities are excluded from the former. Included in the non-productive, or non-economic category are health, social security, culture, education, science, economic chambers, banking, insurance, government bodies and administrative agencies, and social organizations [Yugoslav Survey, Vol. 12, 1971, No. 2, p. 37 fn.]. GNP exceeds SP by an amount that has variously been estimated to range from 10 to 25 percent. OECD estimates of Yugoslavian GNP in recent years have exceeded official Yugoslav statistics of SP by approximately 15 percent. Note that not all services are put in the non-productive category. Services connected with the production of material goods, for example, trade and transport, are included as productive activities. The exclusion of some services from the SP results in a downward bias in the rate of growth of SP in comparison to the growth of GNP.

Table 12 - Selected Economic Indicators, 1952-1973

	Unit	1973	Compound annual growth rate[a]		
			1961/52	1973/61	1973/52
				percent	
Social product	mill. US $	18,014	9.0	6.6	7.6
Per capita social product	US $	859	7.8	5.6	6.5
Industrial value-added	mill. US $	6,623	12.7	8.9	10.5
Total merchandise exports	mill. US $	2,853	10.6	8.6	9.5
Industrial exports[b]	mill. US $	2,466	13.1	11.1	12.0
Total merchandise imports	mill. US $	4,506	10.6	9.0	9.7
Industrial imports[b]	mill. US $	4,088	9.5	9.6	9.6
Industrial employment	thousands	1,665	8.0	3.3	5.3
Population	thousands	20,956	1.1	1.0	1.1

[a]Growth rates computed from values in constant prices. - [b]Industrial exports and imports are defined broadly, e.g. food manufactures and beverages are included.

Source: SZzS [Statistički godišnjak SFRJ, various years].

Table 13 - Structure of Social Product[a], 1952-1973 (percent)

Sector	1952	1956	1961	1965	1973
Public	67.1	65.5	73.0	78.8	81.1
Private	32.9	34.5	27.0	21.2	18.9
Industry	22.0	27.3	29.7	35.6	38.5
Agriculture	33.3	32.2	28.4	22.7	19.5
Forestry	3.9	2.8	1.8	1.6	1.0
Construction	10.6	7.2	9.2	8.9	8.3
Transport and communication	6.5	7.1	7.5	7.4	7.8
Trade and catering	16.5	16.0	17.2	18.1	19.6
Arts and crafts	7.1	7.4	5.7	5.3	5.0

[a]1966 prices. - Totals may not add to 100 because of rounding errors.

Source: SZzS [Statistički godišnjak SFRJ, various years].

Table 14 - Average Annual Compound Growth Rates of Real Gross Domestic Product and Industrial Production, 1950-1970 (percent)

	Real gross domestic product				Industrial production
	total		per capita		
	1960/50	1970/60	1960/50	1970/60	1970/55
Developed market economy countries	4.1	4.9	2.8	3.7	5.1
Developing countries	4.7	5.2	2.4	2.5	7.6
Socialist countries[a]	9.3	6.6	7.8	5.4	9.2
Yugoslavia[b]	7.1[c]	5.9	6.0[c]	4.7	9.9[d]

[a]Excluding non-material services. - [b]Net material product. - [c]1960/52. - [d]Calculated by the author from data in SZzS [Statistički godišnjak SFRJ 1972].

Source: UN [Handbook 1972, Tables 6.2 and 6.7].

Economic instability is evidenced in wide fluctuations in annual growth rates of real social product and industrial production (Table A 7). For example, the yearly growth rates of real social product beginning with 1953 and ending with 1960 were: 20, 1.3, 14.8, -6.0, 23.9, 1.6, 21.6, and 5.8 percent. Poor agricultural performance in 1954, 1956 and 1958 contributed to this instability (the growth of industrial production during this period was much more stable). Bad weather together with vacillating government policy toward agriculture contributed to wide fluctuations in agricultural production (Table A 7). Collectivization policies were strongly resisted by farmers with the result that collectivization was abandoned in 1953. A Land Reform Act followed which limited private holdings of land to 10 hectares. These are examples of agricultural policies during the inaugural stage of development which alternated between increased and relaxed pressures being used to socialize this sector which led to greater and lesser peasant resistance to the policies. The realization that socialization of agriculture could take place only on a voluntary basis was soon reflected in agricultural policy[1]. Abstracting from the agricultural sector, instability of both the social product and industrial production

[1] For more on agricultural policy, see Hoffman, Neal [1962, Chapter 15].

was greater during the reform stage, that is, since 1961, than during the earlier inaugural stage of development. Price and external sector instability have also become greater since 1961 (Tables 22 and A 4).

Causes of the increase in economic instability are not difficult to find. The economy became much more decentralized following 1961, and especially since 1965, than during the previous period when much central control of economic activities remained. As the system became more and more decentralized, the fragmentation of spending and taxing authority made it difficult to achieve a coordinated fiscal policy. Even abstracting from such difficulties, anti-cyclical fiscal policy was not a part of the policy framework. A prominent Yugoslav economist wrote in 1971, "... there is no fiscal policy in Yugoslavia" [Horvat 1971, p. 157]. Fiscal philosophy in Yugoslavia subscribes to the theory that balanced budgets should be maintained. As a result, fiscal policy is pro-cyclical; rising government revenues during an economic boom go hand in hand with increasing government expenditure (or decreasing tax rates - a less likely alternative). And budgets balanced at higher levels are more expansionary than when balanced at lower levels.

Monetary policy is also subject to limitations. The lack of a capital market precludes the use of open market policy. The effects of monetary stringency are resisted by the common enterprise practice of not paying bills when a credit squeeze arises. These defaults on payments tend to feed on themselves and spread throughout the economy until they reach such a magnitude that the restrictive monetary policy is reversed before its intended effects are realized[1]. Defaulting on trade credit extended from one enterprise to another is encouraged by the fact that political bodies almost never allow an enterprise to go bankrupt. This attitude toward bankruptcy stems from the responsibility of the local government for the debts of a bankrupt firm and for minimum wage payments to the enterprise's workers during the bankruptcy proceedings. The employees of a bankrupt firm also add to the local unemployment total thus creating additional problems for local political officials[2]. With fiscal policy virtually non-existent and monetary policy subject to severe institutional limitations, it is not surprising to find that increasing instability accompanied the development of a decentralized, socialist market economy[3].

---

[1] A new law, the Law on Securing of Payments among Users of Public Resources, enacted in late 1975, is expected to severely restrict the growth of interenterprise indebtedness.

[2] For more on monetary policy and non-payment of trade credit, see Tyson [1977].

[3] Monetary and fiscal policy are discussed in Horvat [1971, pp. 130-158]. - Bajt [1971, 1967]. - Dimitrijevic, Macesich [1973]. - World Bank [1975,

Since the centrally planned economic system was abandoned, the economy has become more open as well as more politically and economically decentralized. The movement throughout the period has in general been forward, although at times there have been temporary retreats. The republics, communes and enterprises have all experienced an expansion of their decision-making capacities. The industrial export share of the social product almost tripled during the 21 years to 1973 (from 4.6 to 13.7 percent at current prices and exchange rates). The growth of industrial exports during the same period exceeded the growth of industrial value-added (12.0 vs. 10.5 percent), while the growth of both aggregate merchandise exports and imports exceeded social product growth by more than 25 percent. Yugoslav industrialization has obviously not taken place behind closed doors.

Yugoslavia's experience with central planning of the Soviet-type during the period between the end of World War II and the beginning of the new economic system of workers' management, together with the industry-oriented development strategy which followed, give rise to the hypothesis that the share of industry in Yugoslav gross output is greater than "average" for countries with a similar population and per capita GNP. This hypothesis can be tested by comparing the actual industry share of GNP with a hypothetical share derived from a cross-sectional regression equation in which the parameters were estimated by regressing GNP on population and per capita income[1]. The actual industry share of 20.9 percent in 1952 exceeded the estimated hypothetical share of 12.6 percent by 66 percent. In 1973 the percentage gap between the actual and hypothetical industry shares of 36.1 and 24.8 percent, respectively, had declined to 46 percent (although the percentage point gap between the actual and hypothetical shares widened). Thus the data provide evidence that the economy was "over-oriented" toward industry when the imitative strategy of development was replaced by the workers' self-management system. The decline in the magnitude of the industry bias suggests that the growth of the Yugoslav industrial sector relative to the growth of other economic sectors has been less than expected, based on the experience of other countries. The decrease in the actual industry share may be explained by a diminishing influence of the legacy of the central planning period. Nevertheless, the relative size of the industrial sector remains considerably larger than would be expected from the experience of other countries.

Chapter 11]. - The percentage increase in the money supply during 1970-1974 was as follows: 1970: 19.8, 1971: 14.9, 1972: 42.3, 1973: 36.7, 1974: 26.1 [SZzS, Indeks, Vol. 24, 1975, No. 7, p. 46].

[1] The equation is from Fels, Schatz, Wolter [1971]; data from over 40 countries were used in the estimation of the equation.

1. The "Sources" of Industrial Growth

Industrial production in Yugoslavia has expanded at an annual compound rate exceeding 10 percent since 1952. Petroleum, chemicals and electrical machinery and supplies, have been the fastest growing industrial branches (Table A 8). In this section, the stimulus for industrial growth will be separated into three categories: import substitution, export expansion and domestic demand. This exercise will provide information for analyzing the Yugoslav industrialization strategy with respect to its being "inward" or "outward" oriented[1].

Chenery developed an identity from which the "sources" of growth can be derived. This identity is

$$\Delta X_i = \frac{X_i^1}{Z_i^1} \cdot \Delta D_i + \frac{X_i^1}{Z_i^1} \cdot \Delta E_i + \left(\frac{X_i^2}{Z_i^2} - \frac{X_i^1}{Z_i^1} \right) Z_i^2$$

where

X_i = gross output of industry i

M_i = imports of i

Z_i = $X_i + M_i$ = total available supply

D_i = domestic intermediate and final demand

E_i = exports of i

1, 2 = time periods

By dividing the above equation by X_i, the "sources" of industrial growth can be estimated; the first term on the right of the equality sign is the growth attributable to domestic demand expansion (DD), the second term is growth arising from export expansion (EE), and the last term represents import substitution (IS)[2].

This measure of import substitution is likely to underestimate actual import substitution because intermediate effects are not taken into account. These intermediate effects would be especially important

---

[1] The methodology used here to identify the sources of growth owes its origin to the work of Chenery [1960], and the modifications of Morley, Smith [1970], and Tyler [1973].

[2] This measure has been used in several recent studies, including Ahmad [1968]. - Chenery, Shishido, Watanabe [1962]. - Donges [1973]. - Fane [1971]. - Huddle [1969]. - Lewis, Soligo [1965]. - Steuer, Voivodas [1965].

in Yugoslavia, where there is a relatively high degree of interdependence in the industrial sector. To avoid this downward bias the measure of import substitution can be redefined as follows:

$$IS_i' = \left(\frac{X_i^2}{Z_i'^2} - \frac{X_i^1}{Z_i'^1}\right) Z_i'^2 = \left(\frac{M_i'^1}{Z_i'^1} - \frac{M_i'^2}{Z_i'^2}\right) Z_i'^2$$

where

$$M_i' = \sum_j c_{ij} M_j$$

$$Z_i' = X_i + M_i'$$

with the c_{ij}'s being elements of the Leontief inverse matrix, $(I - A)^{-1}$. Or, in matrix notation:

$$M' = (I - A)^{-1} M$$

a vector of redefined imports. The interpretation of M' is that it is a measure of the domestic production required to completely substitute for imports, assuming final demands remain constant[1].

Similarly, intermediate effects can be taken into account in measuring the contribution of exports to economic growth[2]. Using the same notation as above, the measure of export contribution (EE) is,

$$EE_i' = \frac{X_i^1}{Z_i^1} (E_i'^2 - E_i'^1)$$

and the vector of redefined exports becomes

$$E' = (I - A)^{-1} E$$

which is a measure of the total production attributed to exports. Using

[1] In the calculation of M' only the industrial sector has been considered, i.e., non-industrial imports in the M vector were assigned zero values. The same procedure was used in the calculation of E'.

[2] For an application of this measure, see Tyler [1976, Chapter III], and Stecher [1976, pp. 62 sqq.].

the concepts of redefined exports and imports, the following identity is formulated:

$$\Delta X_i = \frac{X_i^1}{Z_i^{'1}} \Delta D_i + \frac{X_i^1}{Z_i^{'1}} \Delta E_i^{'} + \left(\frac{M_i^{'1}}{Z_i^{'1}} - \frac{M_i^{'2}}{Z_i^{'2}}\right) Z_i^{'2}$$

Again, the proportion of growth attributable to each of the three "sources" can be obtained by dividing through by X_i^1.

The sources of growth were calculated using both constant and current prices. Because Yugoslav prices have been subject to considerable government control and change by decree the use of constant prices is preferred[2]. Since it was not possible to obtain data in constant prices for the 20 branches of the Yugoslav industrial sector, the analysis in this section is limited to the eleven branches for which such data could be obtained (Table 15). To obtain export and import values in constant prices of 1966, current dinar values were arrived at by using the 1966 exchange rate of 12.5 new dinars = US $ 1 and were then deflated by the export or import price index (1966 = 100) for the appropriate branch of industry. Production by industry branch in 1966 prices was calculated by using the 1966 input-output table and

---

[1] The term for domestic demand can be considered as a residual and is found by substracting the sum of IS' and EE' from 100 (percent). Measures of import substitution should be treated with caution. Note that the proportion of growth attributed to import substitution and export expansion is underestimated because the method of calculation does not take account of secondary income effects [see Tyler 1973]. One should also bear in mind that IS' is an ex post concept. It is a definitional measure of import substitution and as such does not necessarily convey implications with respect to an economic policy of import substitution. That is, import substitution as measured here may occur without an orientation of policy in that direction. Additionally, the base years in the measurement have a crucial importance. For example, one would expect, ceteris paribus, that IS' would be less if the end-period (beginning period) year is one of economic buoyancy (slump), and the more rapid the expansion and the closer to full employment the economy is, the less will be IS'. For a discussion of these and other problems associated with measuring import substitution, see Fane [1973]. - Pomfret [1976, pp. 15-25].

[2] Constant price data are, however, not to be considered as being free of imperfections either.

Table 15 - Sources of Industrial Growth[a], 1952-1970 (percent)

	IS	EE	DD	IS	EE	DD	IS	EE	DD
	1952-1956			1956-1961			1961-1965		
Coal and coke	9.1	8.0	83.9	-37.2	19.0	118.2	-8.1	35.4	72.7
Crude petroleum	37.9	7.8	54.3	36.9	9.6	53.5	-1.5	18.6	82.9
Ferrous metals	71.9	15.0	18.1	-67.5	19.7	147.8	21.6	39.5	38.9
Non-ferrous metals	37.2	-13.1	75.9	-55.6	41.1	114.5	18.5	62.8	18.7
Non-metallic minerals	66.6	19.6	13.8	-19.6	19.2	100.4	16.8	36.5	46.7
Metal products	76.6	5.8	17.6	-33.4	18.5	114.9	56.1	20.7	23.2
Electrical machinery, etc.	88.7	8.7	2.6	15.5	17.2	67.3	42.3	15.3	42.4
Chemicals	34.7	9.6	55.7	16.0	11.1	72.9	25.1	21.7	53.2
Paper and paper products	43.4	13.2	55.0	-23.5	16.1	107.4	22.1	20.8	57.1
Textiles	6.3	20.2	73.5	-11.0	13.8	97.2	5.4	21.2	73.4
Food products	7.0	1.8	91.2	- .2	19.8	80.4	5.5	5.5	89.0
Total[b]	36.7	7.8	55.5	-24.8	19.8	105.0	23.0	25.3	51.7
	1965-1970			1952-1961			1961-1970		
Coal and coke	273.0	-82.2	-90.8	- 1.1	13.0	88.1	-430.5	211.7	318.8
Crude petroleum	- 47.3	5.2	142.1	16.7	7.8	75.5	- 31.1	10.1	121.0
Ferrous metals	- 44.6	21.2	123.4	.3	13.1	86.6	- 19.3	26.4	92.9
Non-ferrous metals	-137.9	103.8	134.1	- .3	19.0	81.3	- 62.4	83.0	79.4
Non-metallic minerals	- 55.8	16.1	139.7	13.7	15.5	47.5	- 17.0	24.8	92.2
Metal products	- 94.6	11.4	183.2	.1	10.4	89.5	8.2	15.7	76.1
Electrical machinery, etc.	- 24.5	18.8	105.7	3.5	9.1	87.4	21.4	15.1	63.5
Chemicals	- 10.1	9.0	101.1	1.1	9.1	89.8	11.8	12.8	75.4
Paper and paper products	- 69.1	20.1	149.0	6.3	12.8	80.9	- 11.9	19.4	92.5
Textiles	- 38.3	41.6	96.7	.0	15.9	84.1	- 9.1	28.1	81.0
Food products	- 11.0	4.1	106.9	.1	13.8	86.1	- 2.0	4.7	97.3
Total[b]	- 42.4	21.2	121.2	.7	13.7	85.7	- 28.7	33.3	95.4

[a]Constant price data. - Source of growth attributed to import substitution ≡ IS, to export expansion ≡ EE, to domestic demand ≡ DD. - [b]Weighted average (gross output weights).

Source: See text for method of computation. Calculated from data in: SZzS [Medjusobni odnosi privrednih delatnosti SFRJ 1962 i 1966]. - SZzS [Statistički godišnjak SFRJ, various years]. - SZzS [Statistika spoljne trgovine SFRJ, various years].

indices of production[1].

Looking at the results on a four-period basis (1952-1956, 1956-1961, 1961-1965, 1965-1970) first, import substitution appears to have been an important source of industrial growth in the first and third periods, while being negative in the second and last periods[2]. The increase in the role of import substitution during 1961-1965 coincides with the introduction of a tariff system as part of the economic reforms of 1961. The average tariff rate rose by about 24 percent between 1962 and 1964 (from 18.8 to 23.3 percent) and was accompanied by increasing import restrictions. The last period includes the reform of 1965, in which increasing stress was placed on achieving greater participation in the world economy. The data support the conclusion that progress was indeed made. Helped along by a reduction in the average tariff rate on industrial goods from 26.4 percent in 1964 to 15 percent in 1969 (13.1 percent in 1971), import substitution became significantly negative[3]. Meanwhile the role of export expansion in the growth process declined as export promotion activities were reduced, but still remained at a substantial 21.1 percent.

Dividing the 1952-1970 period into two sub-periods coinciding with the previously defined inaugural and reform stages of development yields a picture of an economy that was becoming substantially more

---

[1] The use of a single input-output table necessitates making the assumption that the product mix, technical coefficients, relative factor prices and relative product prices remain constant throughout the time-period considered. The eleven industry branches for which constant-price calculations were made accounted for about three-fourths of the value-added in 1966 of the industrial sector less electric power and coal and coke. The sources of growth computed from current price data have been included in the Statistical Appendix, Table A 9. Because these results are generally in line with the analysis based on constant prices it was not felt necessary to analyze them here.

[2] A negative value for import substitution implies that imports (direct plus indirect) have grown faster than total supply (imports plus domestic production), i.e., the ratio of imports to total supply was greater at the end of the period than at the beginning. The results for period three provide indication that import substitution and export expansion are not necessarily conflicting sources of growth.

[3] The strange values in Table 15 for the coal industry are connected with a decline in real output from 1965 to 1970. While export expansion in value terms was positive, the negative output expansion produced a negative value for the share of export expansion in output growth.

open[1]. Viewed from this light, import substitution has played a relatively minor role in the growth of industry. During the latter period export expansion assumed greater importance as a source of growth[2]. The economic reforms of the 1960s are thus seen to have been not without success in expanding Yugoslavia's participation in the world economy via import liberalization and export promotion. The import substitution that occurred in 1961-1970 was confined to mainly non-consumer goods industries[3]. Metal products and electrical machinery were the two highest tariff-protected industries in the industrial sector in 1969, the rates being 25.1 and 21.7 percent, respectively; no other industry was protected by a tariff greater than 13.1 percent (Table A 5). Interestingly, some of the more dynamic export industries are also major import substitution industries, e.g., metal products, electrical machinery and chemicals[4].

2. Linkages in the Yugoslav Economy

An important characteristic of an industry is the interdependence between it and other industries. The capacity of an industry to stimulate production increases in supplier and user industries should receive consideration (but should not result in the factor proportions of the production process being ignored) in the formation of development policy[5]. The greater the backward and forward linkages of a sector, the greater, ceteris paribus, will be its contribution to the growth process. In an effort to shed further light on the industrialization process in Yugoslavia, forward and backward linkages have been calculated for 29 economic sectors.

Estimates of the linkages were made using the Leontief inverse matrix $\left[I - A^{(D)}\right]^{-1}$, calculated from the 1962 domestic transactions table. Each of the elements s_{ij} in the matrix indicates the gross do-

---

[1] Calculations based on current price data show that less progress was made in opening the economy, although the direction of movement remained the same.

[2] However, since the economic reforms of the mid-1960s, the growth of exports has slackened, both in absolute terms and in relation to the growth of SP. Merchandise exports and social product (in real terms) grew at an annual compound rate of 11.8 and 8.8 percent respectively during 1956-1965 and 5.4 and 5.8 percent during 1965-1975.

[3] Does not hold true in the case of current price data.

[4] For an argument that import substitution and export expansion are interconnected when considerations of scale economics necessitate production for both the domestic and foreign markets, see Pomfret [1975b].

[5] On linkage considerations in development policy, see Hirschman [1958]. - Yotopoulos, Nugent [1973]. - Riedel [1976].

mestic output of sector i required to sustain a final demand of one unit of sector j. Each column sum, $\sum_i s_{ij}$, represents the gross domestic output from all sectors necessary to produce one unit of final demand of product j. Similarly, each row sum, $\sum_j s_{ij}$, denotes the output of sector i needed for the production of one unit of final demand of each of the j sectors. A measure of the backward linkages of sector i is its column sum, while the forward linkages are indicated by its row sum. Following Rasmussen, one can compute an index of forward and backward linkages[1]. The index relates the linkages of a given sector to what is essentially a national average. The computation of the backward (B_j) and forward (F_i) indexes takes the following form:

$$B_j = \frac{\frac{1}{n} \sum_{i=1}^{n} s_{ij}}{\frac{1}{n^2} \sum_{j=1}^{n} \sum_{i=1}^{n} s_{ij}}$$

$$F_i = \frac{\frac{1}{n} \sum_{j=1}^{n} s_{ij}}{\frac{1}{n^2} \sum_{i=1}^{n} \sum_{j=1}^{n} s_{ij}}$$

where n refers to the number of sectors in the input-output table. The greater the value of B_j and F_i, the greater the stimulus to output in other sectors emanating from a given sector.

Predictably, most manufacturing industries exhibit higher backward linkages than other sectors such as agriculture, forestry and services (Table 16). Ferrous and non-ferrous metals, leather and footwear and food manufactures have the strongest backward linkages. As expected, agriculture displayed substantial forward linkages. In the manufacturing sector, the strongest forward linkages are found in ferrous and non-ferrous metals, metal products and paper.

---

[1] Rasmussen [1956, pp. 133-135]. - Note also that, as implied by the $\left[I - A^{(D)}\right]^{-1}$ matrix, the output figures associated with the s_{ij} elements are domestic requirements.

Table 16 - Backward and Forward Linkages in Yugoslavia, 1962

	Index B_j	Rank		Index F_i	Rank	
		all sectors	industry only		all sectors	industry only
Electrical energy	.90	20.5	17	1.01	13.5	10
Coal and coke	.86	24.5	19.5	1.20	8	6
Crude petroleum	.86	24.5	19.5	1.04	10.5	8
Ferrous metals	1.56	1	1	1.82	1	1
Non-ferrous metals	1.32	2	2	1.58	3	2
Non-metallic minerals	.94	19	16	.85	17	12
Metal products	1.16	5.5	5.5	1.54	4	3
Shipbuilding	1.04	11	10	.61	27.5	20
Electrical machinery	1.16	5.5	5.5	.94	15	11
Chemicals	.99	14.5	12.5	1.21	7	5
Building materials	.97	17.5	14.5	.77	20	14
Wood products	1.11	9	8	1.03	12	9
Paper and paper products	1.13	8	7	1.31	6	4
Textiles	1.06	10	9	1.18	9	7
Leather and footwear	1.20	3	3	.83	18.5	13
Rubber products	.80	26	21	.67	23	16
Food products	1.18	4	4	.66	24.5	17.5
Printing and publishing	.97	17.5	14.5	.65	26	19
Tobacco manufactures	.89	22	18	.66	24.5	17.5
Motion pictures	.99	14.5	12.5	.73	21	15
Miscellaneous manufacturing	1.03	12	11	.58	29	21
Agriculture	1.01	13	.	1.69	2	.
Forestry	.69	28	.	1.01	13.5	.
Construction	1.14	7	.	.91	16	.
Transport and communication	.90	20.5	.	1.35	5	.
Trade and catering	.70	27	.	1.04	10.5	.
Service rendering arts and crafts	.98	16	.	.83	18.5	.
Public utilities	.87	23	.	.61	27.5	.
Scrap and waste	.57	29	.	.70	22	.

Source: Calculated from data in: SZzS [Medjusobni odnosi privrednih delatnosti SFRJ 1962 i 1966].

Spearman rank correlation tests were performed in order to determine if there is an association between the linkage characteristics of industries and certain industrialization variables (Table 17). The correlation between the share of industrial investment (1952-1961) and forward and total linkages is significant at the .01 level, indicating that government policy (the investment decision was a Federal one during this period) had the effect of channelling higher shares of

Table 17 - Spearman Rank Correlation Coefficients between Linkages and Selected Industrialization Variables, 1952-1961

	Backward linkages (B_j)	Forward linkages (F_i)	Total linkages (B_j+F_i)
Annual average output growth[a]	.112	.122	.125
$\frac{IS'}{\Delta X}$[b]	-.241 (-.011)	-.314 (.158)	-.214 (.003)
$\frac{EE'}{\Delta X}$[b]	.364 (.213)	.075 (.184)	.261 (.299)[c]
Annual average export growth[a]	.246	-.295	-.273
Share of industrial investment[d]	.268	.550[e]	.552[e]

[a]17 sectors. - [b]11 sectors, numbers in parentheses are results when current price data were used to compute the sources of growth (20 sectors, see Table A 9). - [c]Significant at .10 level; all others not significant at this level. - [d]21 sectors. - [e]Significant at .01 level.

Source: Computed from data in Tables 15 and 16 and in: SZzS [Statistički godišnjak SFRJ, various years]. - SZzS [Statistika spoljne trgovine SFRJ, various years].

industrial investment toward those industries with the greatest forward and total linkages. In this way output and employment in industries involved in production at a "higher" stage were stimulated. This is in line with the strategy of industrialization that was espoused. The rank correlation between export expansion as a source of growth (computed from current price data) and total linkages is significant at the .10 level; all of the other correlation coefficients were found to be not significant at this level of significance. In addition to the coefficients being not significant, several have the "wrong" sign, for example, the association between import substitution measured in constant prices and linkages turned out to be not only weak but negative. Based on this sketchy analysis, Yugoslav industrialization policy attached importance to linkage characteristics in the allocation of investment funds to specific industrial branches; these branches did not, however, show ex post export expansion and even less import substitution.

3. Labor Force and Employment Considerations

Broad changes in the structure of the economically active population have taken place in the past two decades. Reflecting the rapid growth of the industrial sector, the share of the economically active population in the industrial sector increased over two-fold from 1953 to 1971 - from 8.0 to 17.8 percent of the total economically active population (Table 18). The share of the service sector, encompassing the bulk of the non-industrial, non-agricultural labor force, also increased. The agricultural share in the meantime declined from 66.0 to 43.9 percent. While some progress has been made in shifting labor out of agriculture and into industry, the transfer would have been greater were it not for the capital-intensive bias associated with the workers' self-management system (cf. Chapter I).

Table 18 - Economically Active Persons by Industry, 1953, 1961, 1971

	Thousands of persons			Percent		
	1953	1961	1971	1953	1961	1971
Industry[a]	625	1,138	1,575	8.0	13.6	17.8
Agriculture[b]	5,183	4,675	3,903	66.0	56.1	43.9
Construction	206	318	398	2.6	3.8	4.5
Transport	168	250	323	2.1	3.0	3.6
Trade and catering	220	310	524	2.8	3.7	5.9
Arts and crafts	366	379	434	4.7	4.5	4.9
Other	1,081	1,270	1,733	13.8	15.3	19.4
Total active persons	7,849	8,340	8,890	100	100	100

[a]Including mining. - [b]Including fishing.

Source: SZzS [Statistički godišnjak SFRJ 1970, p. 78; 1974, p. 109].

As revealed in Table 12, industrial employment expanded more rapidly during 1952-1961 than during 1961-1973 (both absolutely and relative to the growth of industrial production)[1]. The pattern of employment growth is related to the change in development strategy that occured in the 1960s. Greater emphasis was placed on increasing the productivity of the industrial labor force, e.g., through capital deepening, as opposed to the earlier strategy in which capital widening was stressed. Quality rather than quantity was emphasized. The greater freedom of enterprise decision-making may also have contributed to the slower growth of industrial employment; the enterprise came in a better position to pursue the maximization goal outlined in Chapter I, which results in a capital-intensive bias. Additionally, changes in the tax system since 1961 encouraged the adoption of labor-saving methods of production. Since the reform of 1965, enterprise taxes have almost exclusively consisted of taxes on the wage bill. According to one Yugoslav economist, this method of taxing enterprises has inflated labor costs by about 60 percent [Horvat 1971, p. 148]. The relative cost of labor was increased further by the dropping of the tax on business capital in 1971.

The reduction in the share of agricultural labor in the total labor force has been aided by the emigration of Yugoslav workers. For example, estimated net worker emigration between 1961 and 1971 totalled 630,000 (Table A 11), while the increase in paid employment came to 792,000, of which 403,000 represented an increase in industrial employment. Thus new jobs originating abroad provided four-fifths as many new employment possibilities as did domestic paid employment. The outflow of workers during this period exceeded the increase in the total labor force, indicating a decline in the domestic labor force. There were almost 1 million more Yugoslavs working abroad in 1975 than in 1965[2]. This figure exceeds the 852,000 increase in the number of jobs provided by the expansion of paid domestic employment. There is about one emigrant worker for every four paid domestic employees. Thus foreign employment has been a strong force in the provision of employment opportunities for Yugoslav workers during the past several years.

---

1 Total paid employment exhibited similar growth characteristics (Table A 10). Paid employment excludes the self-employed, of which the largest numbers are in agriculture, unpaid family workers and apprentices.

2 Data on worker emigration must be treated with caution. Comprehensive records on labor outflow have only recently been kept.

The Yugoslav emigration rate (external migrants as a percentage of total population) of 4.2 percent in 1971 was the second highest in Europe[1]. This outflow of labor has obviously mitigated the problems of providing domestic employment opportunities for workers leaving the agricultural sector[2]. In spite of this, the unemployment problem has been growing (Table A 10). The seriousness of this situation accelerated during the 1960s; registered unemployment in 1967 was 2.5 times the level of 1957[3]. Contributing to the higher level of unemployment were the greater freedom given to the enterprises to pursue the goal of maximizing net income per worker and changes in the tax system noted above[4]. The change in the strategy of development previously cited as well as a deceleration of the rate of economic growth can also be looked upon as contributing factors. While worker emigration may help to alleviate the unemployment problem in the short run, in the long run other solutions must be sought[5].

One response to rising unemployment and worker emigration was the decision taken in 1967 to permit foreign direct investment in Yugoslavia, in the form of joint ventures between Yugoslav enterprises and foreign firms[6]. Foreign investment was seen as contributing to

---

[1] Exceeded only by Portugal; for further details see Baučić [1972]. - About three-fourths of the emigrant workers are unskilled [OECD, Economic Survey 1973, p. 34].

[2] According to 1971 census data, about 45 percent of emigrant workers had been employed in agricultural or related activities prior to departure for foreign employment [SZzS, Statistički godišnjak SFRJ 1971, p. 130].

[3] Included in the Yugoslav definition of unemployment are those registered with the unemployment office although still maintaining a job. Not included in the definition are those receiving unemployment compensation but who have not registered with an unemployment office. See OECD [Economic Survey 1973, p. 29]. - Mase-Lago [1971, pp. 52 sq.].

[4] Some tempering of theoretical conclusions regarding factor ratios employed in worker-managed enterprises may be called for because of political pressures to employ more workers than the enterprise finds optimal (cf. Chapter I). However, in personal conversation with a Yugoslav economist, the opinion was expressed that the problem of redundant workers lessened considerably during the 1960s.

[5] Indeed, return migration, which was negligible prior to the recent severe recession in western Europe, may well accentuate the problem; at any rate, the door to further emigration is now, at least temporarily, being closed, both from the Yugoslav and foreign sides.

[6] There were additional motives behind this decision (cf. Chapter VI).

more rapid economic growth and improved efficiency as well as providing a stimulus to the growth of exports. A strong export orientation must be demonstrated before a proposed joint venture is approved. The expansion of exports, especially manufactured exports, is obviously one way of providing employment opportunities for surplus labor. The employment effects of export expansion will now be examined.

Direct employment (L_{ie}) generated by exports of a particular sector can be calculated by multiplying the direct labor required to produce one unit of the sector's output by the number of units exported[1]. In symbolic form the calculation takes the following form:

$$L_{ic} = \ell_i E_i$$

where

$\ell_i = L_i / X_i$

L_i = employment in industry i in man-years

X_i = value of industry i output

E_i = value of industry i exports

The direct employment effects (L_{Te}) of several sectors, e.g., i = 1, ..., n is then

$$L_{Te} = \sum_{i=1}^{n} \ell_i E_i$$

However, the direct labor required to produce E_i constitutes only part of the total employment generated by E_i. This is because the indirect labor requirements are not taken into account. For example, to produce a given quantity of sewing machines for export requires not only labor employed in the sewing machine industry, but also the labor requirements of the inputs, e.g., steel, purchased from other industries by the sewing machine industry. With the use of a domestic transactions input-output table, these indirect labor requirements can be measured.

---

[1] It is assumed that the labor required to produce a unit of output is the same whether the product is sold domestically or exported.

The total labor, ℓ_i', required to produce a unit of exports (or final demand) of i is calculated as follows:

$$\ell_i' = \sum_i \ell_i \, s_{ij}$$

where

$$s_{ij} = \left[I - A^{(D)}\right]^{-1}_{ij} = \text{element in the inverse Leontief matrix derived from a domestic transactions table}$$

In general terms using matrix notation

$$\ell' = \ell \left[I - A^{(D)}\right]^{-1}$$

where ℓ is a row vector of sectoral labor/output ratios. The vector ℓ' represents the total direct and indirect labor required to produce one unit of final product of each of the sectors. The product of an element of ℓ', say ℓ_i', by the exports of the same sector, E_i, yields the total labor required to produce E_i. Each ℓ_i' is thus an employment multiplier; the employment effect is obtained by multiplying sector i's final demand, or export, change by ℓ_i'. The total labor required to produce the country's aggregate exports is given by

$$L_{Te}' = \ell \left[I - A^{(D)}\right]^{-1} E = \ell' E$$

where E is a column vector of sector exports.

The labor required to produce the exports of each of 29 sectors in 1970 is presented in Table 19. The choice of year was determined by the most recent year for which an input-output table was available. Output and export data used in the calculations were obtained from the 29-sector input-output table of 1970. Employment data were obtained from the Yugoslav statistical yearbook and the author's estimates[1].

[1] Exports of food products appear to be vastly overstated in the input-output table and thus in Table 19. A more plausible value would seem to be about one-half of the 3,185 million new dinars listed in the table. The reduced figure would have the effect of reducing labor requirements of food products exports by about one-half of the amount appearing in Table 19.

Table 19 - Labor Requirements to Produce Exports, 1970

	Direct labor requirements	Total labor requirements	Exports	Export-generated employment	
				direct	total
	man-years per mill. new dinars of output		mill. new dinars	man-years	
1. Electrical energy	8.5528	14.2840	6.129	52	88
2. Coal and coke	21.4680	26.3335	105.547	2,266	2,779
3. Crude petroleum, etc.	6.0997	10.9500	161.553	985	1,769
4. Ferrous metals	7.0751	16.2190	674.830	4,774	10,945
5. Non-ferrous metals	6.7226	13.8335	2,819.130	18,951	38,998
6. Non-metallic minerals	15.8711	23.1713	496.296	7,877	11,500
7. Building materials	12.4517	19.0885	97.534	1,214	1,862
8. Metal products	10.9152	18.3649	2,675.688	29,206	49,139
9. Shipbuilding	7.6184	15.1129	2,547.551	19,408	38,501
10. Electrical machinery, etc.	11.8715	19.9407	1,651.242	19,603	32,927
11. Chemicals	6.6676	13.9790	1,430.911	9,541	20,003
12. Paper and paper products	6.7214	16.5333	466.747	3,137	7,717
13. Wood products	12.9453	22.9206	1,762.529	22,816	40,398
14. Textiles	13.9032	26.9788	2,173.547	30,219	58,640
15. Leather and footwear	10.7839	22.6001	1,050.883	11,333	23,750
16. Rubber products	16.7987	22.9625	102.416	1,720	2,352
17. Food products	3.2645	64.8310	3,184.936	10,397	206,483
18. Tobacco manufactures	11.0900	58.9409	431.899	4,790	25,457
19. Printing, etc.	14.5072	21.8886	59.348	861	1,299
20. Motion pictures	5.4700	9.5549	43.364	237	414
21. Miscellaneous manufacturing	10.3150	24.7100	110.445	1,139	2,729
22. Agriculture	74.6072	112.9520	1,989.201	148,409	224,684
23. Forestry	16.0287	19.7780	300.989	4,824	5,953
24. Construction	8.1836	17.6508	385.050	3,151	6,796
25. Transport and communication	17.1090	21.4888	4,547.296	77,800	97,716
26. Trade and catering	10.6452	12.7799	3,054.756	32,518	39,039
27. Service rendering arts and crafts	23.4957	31.0252	27.395	644	850
28. Public utilities	19.9700	24.5152	.000	0	0
29. Scrap and waste	11.2144	11.2144	48.772	547	547
Total			32,405.984	468,419	953,335
Manufactured export components (1 - 21)			22,052.525	157,649	577,150

Source: Computed from data in: SZzS [Medjusobni odnosi privrednih delatnosti SFRJ 1970]. - SZzS [Statistički godišnjak SFRJ 1972, p. 120]. - Employment data used in the calculation of the agriculture and scrap and waste sectors were estimated by the author.

The domestic employment required to produce total exports in 1970 was equal to about 10 percent of the labor force or 25 percent of paid employment[1]. The labor requirements of manufactured exports amounts to about 6.5 percent of the labor force or 15 percent of paid employment. The data in Table 19 also reveal that about 34,000 dinars (or about US $ 2,300) of exports were needed to generate one employment position. However, the labor requirements indicated in Table 19 do not take into account certain dynamic factors associated with exports. First, the multiplier effect that exports have on the total output of the economy is ignored. Second, the effects of exporting on technological and efficiency advancements are also not taken into consideration.

The growth of the labor force between the two census years of 1961 and 1971 was .6 percent per annum. This means that the labor force has been expanding by around 60,000 members annually. Assuming that labor force additions and the 34,000 dinars of exports associated with one employment position hold fairly stable, then an annual two billion dinar increase in exports would be necessary to absorb the yearly addition to the labor force. An export increase of two billion dinars (of 1970) would imply an increase in real exports of about 5.5 percent currently. Taking the dynamic effects of export expansion into consideration reduces the necessary export growth somewhat. This rate of export expansion is less than has been achieved in the recent past (Table 12).

This exercise has shown that exports are an important source of employment opportunities. The estimates presented above should, however, be considered as only rough approximations. While a full-scale analysis of labor force developments has not been attempted, certain peculiarities in Yugoslavia's labor situation were pointed out, e.g., the emergence of worker emigration as an employment outlet, the maximizing principle of the worker-managed firm and unique taxation characteristics. While progress has been made in rationalizing the sectoral structure of the labor force, more remains to be done. Unemployment has reached an undesirable level. Uncertainties concerning the approximately 1 million Yugoslav workers employed in western Europe (about one-half of whom are working in West Germany) and the future of world trade and commercial policy complicate future prospects. The author's view, however, is that the prospects are good for continued progress in the labor force sphere, especially if efforts to improve Yugoslavia's international competitiveness are reasonably successful. More rapid progress could be made were it

---

[1] See footnote 1, p. 55, for the definition of paid employment. Of course, not all the employment generated by exports was paid employment.

not for the relative over-pricing of labor (and thus under-pricing of capital).

4. Regional Inequalities

The growth of total and industrial product under the system of workers' self-management has been rapid from both an absolute standpoint and in relation to the experiences of other nations. Nevertheless, the country has been unable to overcome a lingering depressed areas problem. Some information on regional economic development is presented in Table 20. Although the areas officially designated as underdeveloped have varied somewhat over time, a good approximation of these "insufficiently developed" areas, as they were termed in the 1966-1970 Five-Year Plan, would include the republics of Bosnia and Herzegovina, Montenegro, Macedonia, and the autonomous province of Kosovo. These regions currently account for about 40 percent of the area, 35 percent of the population and 21 percent of the social product of Yugoslavia.

The social product of the less developed regions (LDRs) approximately doubled between 1959 and 1970, as did the social product of the more developed areas (MDRs). However, a more rapid rate of population growth in the former led to a slower rate of increase of per capita product. Per capita social product in the LDRs grew at an annual compound rate of 4.9 percent from 1959 to 1970, while in the MDRs the rate of increase was 5.8 percent. The situation then is one in which per capita income has been increasing at a reasonably rapid rate in the LDRs, but at the same time the income gap between the rich and the poor regions has been widening.

The government has maintained a goal of achieving a more equal level of income in the various republics and autonomous provinces. The major policy that has been used in attempting to realize this goal has consisted of providing preferential investment treatment to the less developed areas, i.e., these areas were given special preference in the allocation of investment funds and in the rate of interest paid on funds. The goal of the investment policy was to bring about a more rapid growth of the social product in the LDRs than in the country as a whole and thereby a narrowing of the income gap. The ratio of gross fixed investment to the social product during 1953-1969 (Table 20) was 35.0 percent in the LDRs compared to 24.2 in the MDRs. However, in the mid-1960s the role of banks and enterprises as a source of investment funds increased considerably [cf. Chapter III]. With decentralization and the abolishment of the social investment funds,

Table 20 - Some Indicators of Regional Economic Development, 1952, 1959, 1970

		Bosnia and Herzegovina	Montenegro	Croatia	Macedonia	Slovenia	Serbia	Serbia proper	Vojvodina	Kosovo	Less developed regions (LDRs)	More developed regions (MDRs)	Yugoslavia
Population (1, 000)	1952	2, 791	416	3, 913	1, 280	1, 498	6, 900	4, 352	1, 694	780	5, 267	11, 531	16, 748
	1959	3, 185	460	4, 115	1, 377	1, 569	7, 508	4, 763	1, 824	921	5, 943	12, 291	18, 214
	1970	3, 703	525	4, 411	1, 629	1, 718	8, 385	5, 219	1, 946	1, 220	7, 077	13, 294	20, 371
Social product (billion new dinars)[a]	1959	7. 9	. 9	16. 0	3. 0	8. 4	25. 4	16. 4	7. 7	1. 2	13. 7	48. 5	61. 6
	1970	14. 5	2. 4	32. 9	6. 9	19. 4	47. 6	31. 5	13. 6	2. 6	26. 3	97. 4	123. 7
Social product per capita (new dinars)[a]	1959	2, 397	2, 012	3, 879	2, 172	5, 334	3, 377	3, 438	4, 243	1, 349	2, 204	3, 952	3, 349
	1970	3, 925	4, 499	7, 463	4, 223	11, 305	5, 678	6, 030	6, 979	2, 111	3, 716	7, 327	6, 074
Index of social product per capita[a]	1959	100	100	100	100	100	100	100	100	100	100	100	100
	1970	164	223	192	194	212	168	175	164	157	169	185	180
Social product (value-added) in industry (million new dinars)[a]	1952	805	48	2, 151	246	1, 532	2, 195	1, 377	627	192	1, 291	5, 686	6, 977
	1970	5, 469	695	11, 587	2, 238	8, 949	16, 174	11, 332	3, 938	904	9, 333	35, 773	45, 106
Share of industrial value-added[a]	1952	11. 5	. 7	30. 8	3. 5	22. 0	31. 5	19. 7	9. [illegible]	2. 8	18. 5	81. 5	100
	1970	12. 7	1. 5	25. 7	5. 0	19. 8	35. 9	25. 1	8. [illegible]	2. 0	20. 7	79. 3	100
Fixed assets per worker in industry 1952 (1, 000 new dinars)[a]	1952	43. 6	71. 3	.	44. 2	.	.	.	.	52. 4	45. 7	51. 4	50. 2
	1970	109. 8	152. 6	89. 2	84. 2	91. 6	83. 8	79. 0	87. 2	124. 0	108. 2	85. 9	91. 3
Gross fixed investment as percent of the social product[a]	1953-1969	29. 9	52. 6	.	43. 8	.	.	.	.	29. 1	35. 0	24. 2	26. 6
Share of industrial investment	1952	27. 3	3. 3	20. 7	4. 9	14. 6	29. 0	.	.	.	.	.	.
	1970	13. 4	3. 8	19. 8	8. 1	15. 1	39. 8	28. 2	6. 6	5. 0	30. 3	69. 7	100

[a]1966 prices.

Source: SZzS [Statistički godišnjak SFRJ, various years].

the share of gross fixed investment in the social product in the rich and the poor regions has moved closer together. The major remaining investment encouragement instrument is the Fund for Accelerated Development (FAD). The FAD was established in 1965 and is funded by a tax of slightly less than 2 percent of the social product of enterprises in the social sector. The FAD makes loans to the LDRs at concessionary rates. Sectoral allocation of the investment funds is made by the FAD, with the recipient LDR being responsible for allocation at the micro level.

The growth of industrial value-added was more rapid in the LDRs than in the MDRs during 1952-1970, the annual compound growth rates being 11.6 and 10.8, respectively. The LDRs' share of Yugoslav industrial value-added during this period increased from 18.5 to 20.7 percent. Industrial production in Yugoslavia has become considerably more capital-intensive over time, with the trend accelerating since the economic reforms of the 1960s. Factors contributing to this trend have been previously noted in the section on employment trends. Fixed assets per worker in the industrial sector, in thousands of 1966 dinars, stood at 49.2 in 1953, 51.5 (1956), 54.1 (1960), 66.8 (1965) and 91.6 in 1970 [World Bank 1975, p. 61]. But whereas in 1952 fixed assets per worker in industry in the MDRs exceeded that in the LDRs by about 12 percent, by 1970 this relationship had turned around and fixed assets per industrial worker in the LDRs were about 25 percent greater than in the MDRs. This implies that either investment in the LDRs was directed toward relatively capital-intensive industries to a greater extent than in the MDRs or else production for given industries was more capital-intensive in the LDRs. The former explanation explains at least part of the difference in capital-intensity; more than 52 percent of the industrial investment in the LDRs during 1952-1969 was in the four industries of coal mining, ferrous and non-ferrous metals and non-metallic minerals as compared to only 30 percent in the MDRs [World Bank 1975, p. 198]. These industries, with the exception of the latter, have relatively high fixed assets per worker (see Table A 14). This pattern of investment is at least partially attributable to the differing natural resource endowments of the regions. It also seems likely, however, that the relative labor abundance of the LDRs has not been fully exploited. J. Plummer in a recent study estimated that the 1962 level and composition of industrial production could have been achieved with 81.0 percent of the actual capital used. On a North-South regional division, industrial production in the Northern republics could have been achieved with an estimated 85.3 percent of the actual capital and in the Southern republics with 78.0 percent of the actual capital [Plummer 1970, Table II].

5. The Structure of Industrial Enterprises According to Size

It is well known that the size of the firm has implications regarding economic efficiency (both static and dynamic). Thus an examination of the size structure of a nation's industrial sector can provide information concerning the efficiency of industrial production. An examination of the size structure of Yugoslav industrial enterprises reveals that the number of enterprises rose from 2,330 in 1953 to 2,773 in 1972 (Table 21)[1]. Although the total number of enterprises in 1972 was somewhat larger than in 1953, there has been a considerable decrease in the number and share of small enterprises (125 or less employees) during this period. The share of firms in this category declined from 64.9 percent of industrial enterprises in 1953 to 39.5 in 1961 and 30.8 in 1972. The share of industrial employment, fixed assets and social product associated with small enterprises has also decreased[2]. Only about 3 percent of industrial workers were employed by these small firms in 1970. This pattern of change in the size structure of industrial enterprises has probably been a positive factor in the industrial growth in Yugoslavia in that it made increases in production efficiency possible through the realization of economies of scale.

The predominance of large enterprises is greater than would be expected in a country at Yugoslavia's stage of development. This large firm orientation can be expected to affect efficiency in two principal ways. The possibility of realizing greater economies of scale would have a positive effect on efficiency. On the other hand, larger and fewer firms imply greater monopoly power and increase the likelihood of collusion. The largest industrial enterprise in Yugoslavia, the oil concern INA, has assets that are less than 2 percent of those of Standard Oil Company of New Jersey, the largest United States oil firm. The United States Steel Corporation is fifty times as large as Yugoslavia's largest steel enterprise[3]. The scope for monopoly power is very real, however, since the domestic market in Yugoslavia is much smaller than that of the United States. Nevertheless, the orienta-

---

[1] A large decrease in the number of enterprises took place after World War II; there were 3,254 enterprises in 1939.

[2] The data in Table 21 actually understate the importance of large enterprises. This is because it is common for Yugoslav industrial enterprises to become members of groups of firms in which certain enterprise functions are centralized.

[3] The comparisons are from Dirlam, Plummer [1973, p. 75].

Table 21 - Industrial Enterprises According to Numbers Employed, 1953, 1961, 1972

Industrial sector characteristic	Total	Enterprise distribution according to number of persons employed (percent)								
		less than 16	16-29	30-60	61-125	126-250	251-500	501-1,000	1,001-2,000	more than 2,000
Number of enterprises										
1953	2,330	13.1	11.8	18.6	21.4	15.0	10.3	5.6	4.7	4.7
1961	2,787	3.3	4.4	10.3	21.5	21.8	18.1	11.5	5.8	3.2
1972	2,773	5.8	3.3	6.3	15.4	20.4	19.7	14.2	9.4	5.9
Number of employees										
1961	1,137,737	.7	.2	1.2	4.7	9.6	15.7	19.8	19.8	28.9
1972	1,617,715	.1	.1	.5	2.4	6.4	12.1	17.2	22.1	29.1
Active fixed assets (purchase value, m. ND[a])										
1961	26,871	less than .1	.2	1.6	5.7	8.4	16.0	18.4	17.9	33.8
1972	197,041	less than .1	.1	.6	3.0	6.5	14.1	13.1	19.6	37.9
Social product (m. ND[a])										
1961	14,237	.1	.2	1.1	3.9	8.1	13.6	19.9	22.9	30.2
1972	88,588	.2	.2	.7	2.7	6.3	12.1	16.7	22.0	39.2

[a] Million new dinars in current prices.

Source: SZzS [Statistički godišnjak SFRJ 1954, 1963, 1974, Tables 112, 109.5, 109.5, respectively].

tion of Yugoslav industry toward the relatively large enterprise has probably been a positive factor in industrial growth and resource efficiency, although abuse of monopoly power is not rare. Worthy of consideration here is Vanek's argument that the optimum size of firm tends to be smaller and the structure of industry more competitive in a labor-managed system than in other types of market economies (Yugoslav enterprises, as noted above, do not appear so large when compared with firms in the industrialized countries) [Vanek 1970, p. 272]. The fulfillment of the competitive characteristic requires ease of entry, a condition which is less than satisfactory in Yugoslavia (due in large measure to the influence of existing enterprises on bank lending policies).

Chapter V: Growth and Structural Change in the External Sector

The Yugoslav external sector has undergone vast changes, in value and composition, during the first two decades in which the system of workers' self-management has been operative. In this chapter further information on the effects of previously discussed policies is provided as growth and structural change of foreign trade are examined. While imports are considered to some extent, the major concern is with exports. To provide a general perspective of the changes that have occurred, the current account of the balance of payments is examined in the following section. This is followed by an analysis of structural change at the one-digit SITC level and in terms of the Yugoslav broad classification of exports and imports according to end use and stage of production. Structural change at this level of aggregation has been more pronounced in the export sector than has been the case with imports. The manufactured export share of total exports has grown rapidly, as have the shares of capital goods exports and exports of finished goods. Imports of manufactured goods have also grown more rapidly than imports of primary goods. Supply bottlenecks have stimulated imports of intermediate goods, especially in the latter half of the period.

Export growth is then examined in a constant-market-shares framework, in which the expansion of exports is related to the growth of world trade, commodity and market structures and a residual competitive effect. Changes in the pattern of trade in manufactured goods are then examined. The structure of trade in industrial products is analyzed from four standpoints: cumulative capital and labor requirements, comparative advantage and net exports and imports by industrial branch, hypothetical and "revealed" comparative advantage, and the contribution of the various industry branches to the incremental value of industrial exports. The industrialization strategy of emphasizing the development of industries producing finished goods relative to primary and semi-manufactured industries is reflected in the structure of exports. A somewhat mixed picture develops when the composition of exports is related to the factor intensiveness of production.

In a following section direct and indirect import requirements of production for 29 economic sectors are shown. These data point toward increasing import requirements of production. This tendency is especially evident in the case of industrial exports and investment. Following the analysis of import requirements, exports on a value-added basis are calculated. The value-added measure of exports provides important insights into the supply orientation of export earnings and the net balance-of-payments effects of exports by industry branch. The geographical structure of exports is examined in the penultimate section. Exports to eastern Europe are shown to be more volatile than exports to the EEC. Manufactured goods weigh more heavily in exports to eastern Europe and the developing countries than in exports to the EEC. In the final section export supply factors are examined.

1. Balance of Payments

A useful introduction to the foreign sector of the Yugoslav economy is provided by an examination of the balance of payments[1]. It is not surprising to find that the merchandise trade balance has been negative in every year from 1946 to 1973 (Table 22); the needs of a relatively underdeveloped country for imports of capital goods and primary and intermediate materials during the course of rapid industrialization are well-known[2]. In only four postwar years have merchandise exports exceeded 75 percent of imports. In contrast to the trade balance, the balance on services and unilateral transfers has been positive throughout the postwar period. This positive balance has occasionally outweighed the trade deficit to produce a current account surplus.

Remittances from emigrants and workers abroad and tourist earnings have been especially dynamic in the last decade. The surplus on the private transfers and worker remittances account increased from $ 48 million in 1961 to $ 1, 512 million in 1973. This rapid growth of net earnings resulted mainly from a rapid rise in worker remittances beginning in the mid-sixties. The value of these remittances was about $ 900 million in 1972 and exceeded $ 1.25 billion in 1973. The net receipts from foreign travel reached $ 350 million in 1973, having risen from $ 44 million in 1963. Tourism earnings should maintain their buoyancy over the long term, despite occasional interruptions such as occurred during the recent world recession. Earnings from worker remittances cannot be expected to continue their growth pattern as the doors to further labor immigration are being closed tighter and

[1] The analysis is restricted to the current account of the balance of payments, i.e., that part which is directly related to current national income.

[2] During the interwar period the balance of trade was consistently in surplus (cf. Chapter II).

Table 22 - Yugoslav Balance of Payments on Current Account, 1938-1973 (million US $)

Year	Trade balance			Services and unilateral transfers				Current account balance	Export/ import ratio
	total	exports f.o.b.	imports c.i.f.	total	private transfers and workers' remittances[a]	official	others		
1938	4	103	- 99	5	.	-	5	9	1.04
1946	- 211	58	- 269	239	.	225	14	28	.22
1947	- 106	173	- 279	123	.	98	25	17	.62
1948	- 55	323	- 378	72	.	54	18	18	.85
1949	- 140	193	- 333	46	.	21	25	- 94	.58
1950	- 124	165	- 289	42	.	25	17	- 82	.57
1951	- 246	192	- 438	281	.	187	94	35	.44
1952	- 140	234	- 394	134	.	102	32	- 6	.59
1953	- 229	192	- 421	165	.	139	26	- 64	.46
1954	- 120	247	- 367	124	.	90	34	4	.66
1955	- 204	266	- 470	138	.	83	55	- 66	.57
1956	- 166	329	- 495	170	.	92	78	4	.66
1957	- 275	401	- 674	164	.	56	105	-111	.59
1958	- 236	469	- 699	147	.	44	103	- 89	.67
1959	- 275	487	- 704	138	.	49	89	- 79	.69
1960	- 269	576	- 845	147	48	55	44	-122	.68
1961	- 346	583	- 929	129	48	34	47	-217	.63
1962	- 199	701	- 900	151	57	25	70	- 48	.78
1963	- 278	802	-1,080	198	102	5	91	- 80	.74
1964	- 433	895	-1,328	230	106	20	104	-203	.67
1965	- 195	1,094	-1,289	265	59	30	176	70	.85
1966	- 351	1,225	-1,576	312	98	11	203	- 39	.77
1967	- 454	1,253	-1,707	379	160	12	207	- 75	.73
1968	- 532	1,265	-1,797	437	191	11	230	95	.70
1969	- 659	1,475	-2,134	596	284	2	310	- 63	.69
1970	-1,195	1,673	-2,874	848	544	1	303	-342	.58
1971	-1,435	1,817	-3,252	1,078	789	- 1	290	-357	.56
1972	- 992	2,237	-3,233	1,411	1,049	- 1	363	419	.69
1973	-1,576	2,824	-4,400	2,010	1,512	- 2	500	434	.64

[a] Prior to 1966, emigrant and worker remittances.

Source: SZzS [Statistika spoljne trgovine SFRJ, various years]. - OECD [Economic Survey 1974, Table I]. - Pertot [1971, annexed table].

tighter by one western European country after another[1].

[1] The Federal Republic of Germany banned additional labor immigration in 1973, France in 1974. Some countries, e.g., Sweden and the Netherlands, have resorted to indirect measures such as the enforcement of complicated laws and union agreements, in the name of "progressive social legislation", to still the inflow of foreign workers. For an interesting account of a Yugoslav worker and his family in Sweden see Kramer [1976].

A 67 percent increase in imports (21 percent in real terms) in 1974 together with a 33 percent rise in exports (1 percent in real terms) produced a visible trade deficit of over $ 4 billion. Faced with this large trade deficit and diminishing prospects for the service account, Yugoslavia introduced an import deposit scheme and tightened foreign exchange allotments. Further changes in the import regime are being planned in order to reduce the country's dependency on imports.

2. Structural Change in Foreign Trade: Broad Classification

Dramatic changes in the structure of exports and imports have taken place during the course of the last two decades. In this section these changes are examined at a highly aggregative level. Structural changes of exports and imports classified according to SITC sections are examined first. Following this, Yugoslav end use and stage of production classifications serve as the basis for an examination of broad structural changes.

a. Structural Change in the Composition of Foreign Trade: Classification According to SITC Sections

As industrialization proceeds certain structural changes in foreign trade can be expected to take place. Historical evidence indicates that the share of manufactured exports in total exports is positively associated with per capita income and the degree of industrialization[1]. The bases of the relationship are well known (e.g., changes in the composition and supply of factors of production, scale, learning and technology factors and spillover effects) and will not be dealt with here. Structural changes within the manufactured export sector can also be expected to accompany industrialization. The share of finished manufactures in total manufactured exports tends to rise while the share of exports of semi-finished goods tends to fall.

In so far as the structure of imports is concerned, the hypothesis is advanced that the share of manufactured imports in total imports rises with industrial development. While the historical evidence concerning the association between industrialization and import structure is somewhat mixed, Yugoslavia's rather small domestic market provides a relatively large scope for manufactured imports in contrast to countries with large domestic markets in which the efficient production of a wider range of goods is more likely.

---

[1] See, for example, Maizels [1963]. - Kuznets [1964]. - Banerji [1972].

Information on what has actually happened to the structure of Yugoslav exports and imports is found in Figures 4 and 5 and Table A 12. The shares of manufactured goods (SITC 5-8) and primary commodities (SITC 0-4) in total exports were completely reversed by 1970 in contrast to 1952 and thus moved in the hypothesized direction. Whereas manufactured goods accounted for 29.1 and primary commodities 69.9 percent of total exports in 1952, the respective shares were 72.9 and 26.6 percent in 1973. The Yugoslav share of world exports of SITC 5-8 rose from .20 percent in 1952 to .60 percent in 1972. The Yugoslav share of total world exports during the same period increased from .31 to .54 percent[1]. The increasing importance of manufactures in Yugoslav exports is reflective of the policy of increasing per capita income via industrialization and the concomitant effect on exports as well as of manufactured export promotion measures[2]. Consistent with the above hypothesis that the growth of exports of finished manufactures outpaces that of semi-finished manufactures is the marked increase in the shares of SITC sections 7 and 8 (machinery and miscellaneous manufactures) in total exports in contrast to the change of the shares of sections 5 and 6 (chemicals and manufactured goods classified by material). In 1952 sections 5 and 6 accounted for 28.4 percent of total exports with the share of sections 7 and 8 being .6 percent. In 1973 sections 5 and 6 made up 34.7 percent of total exports, while the share of sections 7 and 8 was 38.1 percent (Table A 12).

While the shift in the structure of Yugoslav exports appears dramatic, it is not untypical for an industrializing nation. In Table 23 are found the shares of manufactures (SITC 5-8) in total exports of five southern European semi-industrialized countries in 1953 and 1971. When viewed in relation to the other countries in the table, the structural change

---

[1] The share was about .57 in both 1938 and 1948. Total exports declined in 1949 and did not again reach the level of 1948 until 1956. Export growth during 1948-1956 was influenced by an economic blockade of Yugoslavia imposed by the Soviet bloc countries (see section 5 of this chapter). A peak of .60 percent of world exports was reached in 1966. The Yugoslav share of world manufactured exports (SITC 5-8) reached a peak of .63 percent in 1965.

[2] The share of industry in the social product rose from 22 percent in 1952 to 38 percent in 1972 (measured in 1966 prices). The proportion of industrial output (including the energy branches) exported rose from 4.6 percent in 1952 to 13.9 percent in 1972 (see Table 26). A discussion of export policy can be found in Chapter III.

Figure 4 - Structure of Yugoslav Exports According to SITC 5-8 and 0-4, 1952, 1962, 1972

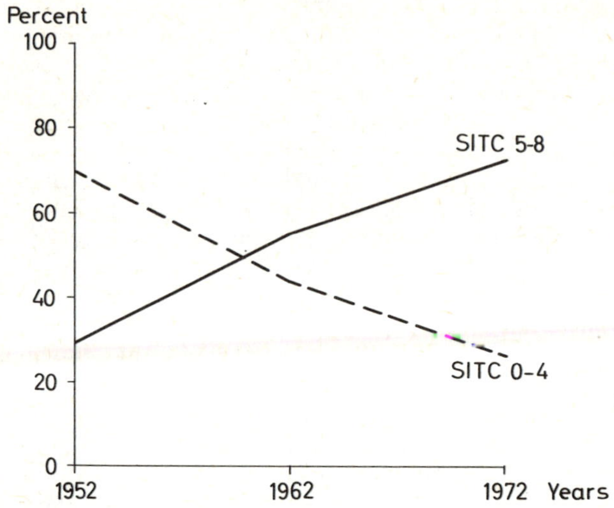

Source: Table A 12.

Figure 5 - Structure of Yugoslav Imports According to SITC 5-8 and 0-4, 1952, 1962, 1972

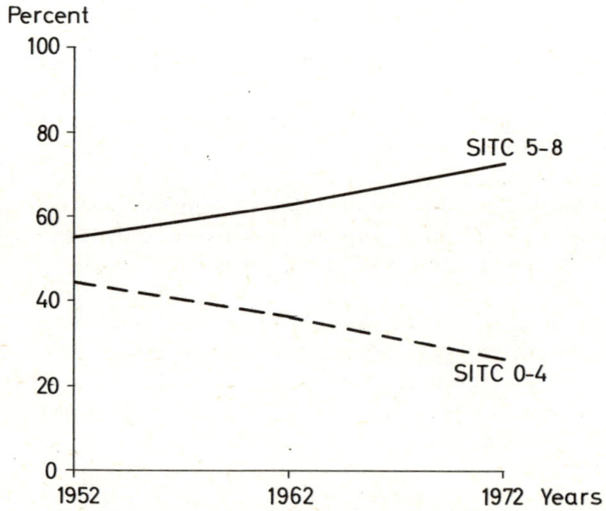

Source: Table A 12.

in Yugoslav exports in terms of manufactures and primary commodities does not appear so enormous.

The export structure of Yugoslavia is tilted more toward manufactures than is its commodity production. A comparison of column 3 in Table 23 with either column 2 or 4 (the definition of manufactured exports in these two columns is not identical) reveals that Yugoslavia's manufactured export performance in relation to its degree of industrialization compares favorably with this group of countries. Whether this success is primarily the result of skilled policy-making or luck (e.g., in terms of resource base and location) is an important and difficult question; it is hoped that this study will help to answer it.

Table 23 - Shares of Manufactures in Total Exports and Value-Added in Manufacturing as Percentage of Value-Added in Commodity Production of Five Southern European Countries (percent)

	Share of SITC 5-8 in total exports (percent)		Gross value-added in manufacturing as percent of value-added in commodity production	Manufactured exports as percent of merchandise exports[a]
	1953	1971	1970	1969
Greece	9.6	38.1	45.3	49.79
Portugal	38.3	66.4	65.4	79.55
Spain	15.6	61.4	61.9	62.29
Turkey	3.9	12.6	31.9[b]	12.28
Yugoslavia	37.9	72.8	58.0	74.41

[a]UNCTAD total A. - [b]1968.

Source: Columns 1-2: UN [Yearbook 1956, 1971]. - Columns 3-4: Morawetz [1974, Table 1].

As was hypothesized, structural changes on the import side have been less dramatic than has been the case with exports. The direction of change has followed that of exports, i.e., imports of manufactured goods have increased in relative importance. The share of SITC sections 5-8 in total imports stood at 69.4 percent in 1973, after being

55.3 percent in 1952. The big gainer here was imports of processed industrial supplies. Despite this growth, Yugoslav industrial enterprises have frequently suffered from shortages of supplies; economic policy which worked to the disadvantage of industries producing industrial supplies contributed to these bottlenecks.

b. Structural Change in the Composition of Foreign Trade: End Use and Stage of Production Classifications

Exports and imports can also be grouped according to end use and stage of production[1]. An examination of exports classified by end use reveals that exports of capital goods, after being less than one-tenth of one percent of total exports in 1952 (as well as in 1951, the first year in which these goods were exported in any quantity) reached a peak of 18 percent in 1962 and 1966 (Table A 13). Since 1966, exports of raw materials and semi-manufactures have increased from 43 to 53 percent of total exports, while the share of exports of capital goods fell to 14 percent and exports of consumer goods declined from 39 to 33 percent of total exports. This tendency approximately coincided with the reforms of the mid-1960s, in which an export structure more closely reflecting the nation's comparative advantage was introduced as a major policy objective.

The major category of capital goods exports is transport equipment (ships, automobile products and railway vehicles are the leading export items in this group) followed by electrical and non-electrical machinery. Among the developing and semi-industrialized countries, Yugoslavia is one of the principal exporters of capital goods. The share of capital goods in total manufactured exports is greater in Yugoslavia than in six other southern European industrializing nations, included in which are both capitalist and socialist economies[2]. The rise in importance of exports of capital goods reflects the relatively favorable

---

[1] Yugoslavia publishes data on exports and imports classified according to end use (raw materials and semi-manufactures, capital and consumer goods; in Yugoslav terminology the categories are termed reproduction, investment and consumer goods) and stage of production (raw materials, semi-finished and finished goods; according to Yugoslav terminology these groups are referred to as crude, simply transformed and more elaborately transformed articles). These classifications differ from those of the United Nations; they are presented here as another way of observing broad structural changes in Yugoslav foreign trade.

[2] UN [Economic Bulletin, Vol. 20, 1968, No. 2, p. 48]. - The countries included in the comparison, in addition to Yugoslavia, are Greece, Portugal, Spain, Turkey, Rumania and Bulgaria.

attention this industry has received from economic policy-makers (cf. Chapter III). Moreover, the metal-using sector, especially the automotive industry, is where the bulk of industrial cooperation agreements and joint ventures have taken place (cf. Chapter VI)[1].

When exports are classified according to stage of production, it is again clear that a vast change in composition has taken place (Table A 13). The shift from exports of raw materials and semi-finished goods to finished goods has been particularly extensive. Exports of raw materials and semi-finished goods made up 93 percent of total exports in 1952, with the share of finished goods exports being only 7 percent; in 1961 the respective shares were 63 and 37 percent. In 1973 exports of raw materials had fallen to 9 percent of total exports (from 50 percent in 1952 and 25 percent in 1961), exports of semi-finished goods declined to 35 percent of total exports (from 43 percent in 1952 and 38 percent in 1961), while exports of finished goods had risen to 57 percent of total exports (from 7 percent in 1952 and 37 percent in 1961). This trend reflects the industrialization strategy of increasing the level of domestic processing as well as emphasizing the production of an extremely wide range of products. There have also been efforts to achieve a diversified foreign trade structure, from both the country and commodity standpoints. The rationale behind this policy, undertaken at both the government and enterprise levels, is that, by minimizing risk and increasing flexibility, diversification reduces export price and earnings fluctuations[2].

Considerable success in diversifying exports has been achieved. Using the Hirschman measure of commodity concentration, Zoran Trputec found the coefficient of commodity concentration of Yugoslav exports to be 34.05, 21.40 and 17.49 in 1945, 1954 and 1968, respectively[3]. The coefficients are low (indicating a high degree of diversification) by world standards, and especially so when compared with other less developed and semi-industrialized countries. A United Nations study

---

[1] Only a limited number of joint venture projects have become operational, however.

[2] A theory of "capillary trade", as this type of trade strategy has been called by the Yugoslav economist, Vladimir Pertot, appeared in Yugoslavia; for a further discussion see Horvat [1971, p. 122]. - World Bank [1975, pp. 276 sq.]. - Neuberger [1968, pp. 363-366]. - Neuberger suggests that Yugoslavia's highly diversified export structure may be a legacy of the system of central planning.

[3] Trputec [1973, p. 122]. - On the calculation of the coefficient of concentration see Hirschman [1945]. - For an application of this measure of concentration see Michaely [1962].

showed that Yugoslav exports in 1968 were less concentrated than those of any of the developing and semi-industrialized countries for which the coefficient of commodity export concentration was calculated, and also less than all but three of the developed countries (over 100 countries in all) [UN, Handbook 1972].

Turning briefly to the Yugoslav twenty-branch industrial sector, indications are that the trend toward greater export diversification has not been confined to total exports; not unexpectedly, a similar movement is observed for manufactured exports. The number of seven-digit items exported within SITC 5-8 increased from 737 in 1961 to 1,483 in 1971 [World Bank 1975, p. 276]. Further evidence of increasing manufactured export diversification is found in an examination of the industry branches which have an above-average share (greater than 5 percent) of the exports of the industrial sector. The number of these greater-than average exporters totaled 4 in 1952, 7 in 1962 and 8 in 1972 (Table 25). The four "export branches" in 1952 consisted of the traditional non-ferrous metals, wood products, food manufactures and tobacco industries. Metal products, electrical machinery and supplies, shipbuilding and textiles had joined the list of "export branches" by 1962. The metal products industry, which became the leading export industry, has been cited as an example of an industry whose growth was of an import-substituting character and whose export expansion came about "by unrestricted export incentives and reckless depreciation of the dinar and by taking capital from other industries to finance buyers abroad" [Fabinc 1972]. The addition of the chemical and leather and footwear industries in 1972 reflects in part a greater utilization of domestic raw materials, e.g., hides, non-ferrous metals and non-metallic minerals.

Import structure by end use, since it settled into a degree of stability in 1954, has shown a tendency for raw materials and semi-manufactured goods to increase in importance, while the opposite trend is observed for consumer goods, as the domestic consumer goods industry developed. Food imports declined from 24 percent of total imports in 1954 to 8 percent in 1973; meanwhile the share of imports of consumer durables, with their relatively high income elasticity of demand, was rising. Imports of capital goods have tended to remain, with some exceptions, at around one-fifth of total imports. In so far as imports by stage of production are concerned, there has been a downward trend in recent years in the share of raw materials. Interestingly, however, the structure of imports by stage of production in 1973 was quite similar to the pre-war structure of 1939.

In summary, the foreign trade structure of Yugoslavia, in terms of highly aggregative commodity bundles, has undergone vast change in the course of the industrialization that has taken place since the introduction of the system of workers' self-management. The shift in exports toward more highly-processed goods has been especially pronounced. Associated with the increase in the share of industry in the social product from 22.0 to 38.5 percent between 1952 and 1973 has been a rise in the manufactured export proportion of total exports from 58.7 to 86.4 percent. A relative increase in imports of manufactured goods has also taken place, albeit on a smaller scale. The share of manufactured imports in total imports rose from 83.0 to 90.6 percent between 1952 and 1973[1]. The commodity concentration of total and manufactured exports decreased over time. This increase in export diversification continued following the economic reform of 1965, which placed great emphasis on specialization on the basis of comparative advantage.

c. A Constant-Market-Shares Analysis of Export Growth

In this section an investigation of the growth of exports during 1961-1965 and 1965-1972 is undertaken with the purpose of estimating the relative quantitative importance of various factors affecting this growth. Among the goals of the reforms of 1961 and 1965, but especially the latter, was to improve Yugoslavia's participation in the international division of labor. Although the reforms were discussed in Chapter III, it is useful to point out again that included in the foreign trade objectives of the 1965 reform were the following: to achieve a broader integration into the international division of labor, to do away with budget subsidies for exports, to subject the domestic market to greater competitive pressures from abroad, and to assure a much faster growth of exports over production [see Anakioski 1969, p. 71].

The method used here to assess the factors working on Yugoslavia's export growth is the constant-market-shares analysis. This method is a useful, albeit simplified method for examining the growth of exports[2]. Export growth is attributed to four factors: the growth of world

---

[1] A broader definition of manufactured exports and imports than that associated with SITC 5-8 is used here, e.g., food manufactures and beverages are included as manufactured exports and imports.

[2] For a fuller discussion of the theory of the constant-market-shares analysis see Tyszinski [1951]. - Leamer, Stern [1970, Chapter 7]. - Richardson [1971]. - For recent applications of constant-market-shares analysis see, Donges [1973]. - Girgis [1973]. - Pomfret [1976, pp. 60 sqq.]. - Tyler [1976, pp. 117-122]. - Banerji [1974].

trade, commodity structure, market structure, and a residual which has been termed the competitive effect. Various influences may be subsumed within the competitive effect, for example, movements in relative prices, quality and marketing factors, and government policies.

The constant-market-shares analysis adopts the norm that a country's share in world export markets should remain constant over time. The difference between the hypothetical growth of exports implied by this norm and the actual growth is then broken down into commodity, market and competitive effects. The application of the constant-market-shares analysis to the growth of Yugoslav exports proceeds from the following identity:

$$E^2 - E^1 = rE^1 + \sum_i (r_i - r) E_i^1 + \sum_i \sum_j (r_{ij} - r_i) E_{ij}^1$$
$$+ \sum_i \sum_j (E_{ij}^2 - E_{ij}^1 - r_{ij} E_{ij}^1)$$

where

E^1 = value of total merchandise exports of Yugoslavia in the initial year

E^2 = value of Yugoslav exports in the end year

E_{ij} = value of Yugoslav exports of commodity i to market j

E = $\sum_i \sum_j E_{ij}$

r = percentage increase in total world exports between years 1 and 2

r_i = percentage increase in world exports of commodity i between years 1 and 2

r_{ij} = percentage increase in world exports of commodity i to market j between years 1 and 2

The actual increase in Yugoslavia's exports appears on the left of the identity sign $E^2 - E^1$. The four terms on the right side represent the world trade effect (hypothetical increase in Yugoslav exports required to maintain her share of world exports), commodity composition effect (increase in exports resulting from a favorable commodity structure), market distribution effect (export growth resulting from a favorable market structure), and the residual competitive effect, respectively. Seven commodity categories, twelve markets and two time periods were used in applying the constant-market-shares analysis to Yugoslav export growth[1]. The 1965 dividing point was used because it was the economic reform of 1965 which emphasized most strongly the goal of increasing the international competitiveness of the economy and more actively participating in the international economy.

An examination of the results (Table 24) reveals the competitive effect, accounting for 58.8 percent of the increase in exports, to have been the major force in the export expansion that took place during 1961-1965, followed by the world trade effect of 42.8 percent. The commodity and market structures of exports were not important ex-

Table 24 - Constant-Market-Shares Analysis of Yugoslav Export Growth, 1961-1965, 1965-1972

	Yugoslav exports[a]			
	1961-1965		1965-1972	
	mill. US $	percent	mill. US $	percent
Increase in exports	522.5	100	1,146.0	100
Increase due to:				
World trade effect	233.5	42.8	1,322.7	115.4
Commodity composition effect	-10.4	-2.0	-44.2	-3.8
Market distribution effect	2.3	.4	-100.8	-8.8
Competitive effect	307.1	58.8	-31.7	-2.8

[a]Yugoslav exports (mill. US $): 1961: 568.8, 1965: 1,091.3, 1972: 2,237.3.

Source: Calculated from data in OECD [Trade by Commodities 1961, 1965, 1972]. - UN [Monthly Bulletin, September 1974]. - UN [Handbook 1972].

[1] The commodity groups were SITC sections 0 + 1, 2 + 4, 3, 5, 6 + 8, 7 and 9. The market regions were the EEC, EFTA, Eastern Europe, other Europe, United States, Canada, Developing America, Developing Africa, Japan, Socialist Asia, other Asia, and all other.

planatory factors in the growth of exports. However, the picture differed considerably in the second period. The major change during 1965-1972 was in the magnitude of the competitive effect, as it became a negative influence. The world trade effect soared to three digits, while specialization in commodities for which there was a relatively slow growing world demand and in markets that were growing relatively slowly acted as mild hindrances to export growth.

The greater world trade effect in the more recent period is explained by a reduction in the growth of Yugoslav exports in relation to world export growth. Whereas in 1961-1965, the growth of Yugoslav and world exports was 91.9 and 39.3 percent respectively (17.7 and 8.6 percent on a compound annual growth basis), the comparative export growth figures in 1965-1972 were 105.0 and 121.2 percent (10.8 and 12.0 percent compound annual rates). It is the reason for this failure to keep up with the growth of world trade that will explain much of the change in the pattern of export growth factors that took place in 1965-1972. Although the commodity and market structures in 1965 were less favorable than in 1961 relative to world trade trends in the seven years following 1965 and four years following 1961, the crucial change was the decline in the broadly-defined competitiveness factor.

To what extent was the decrease in "competitiveness" a function of government policy? A complete analysis of this question will not be attempted; however, some general observations are in order. The rate of growth of Yugoslav exports failed to exceed world export growth in four of the seven years beginning with 1966 and ending with 1972 (the Yugoslav growth rate was greater than the world growth rate in each of the years 1962-1965). The particularly troublesome years for Yugoslav exports were 1967 and 1968, when total exports grew by 2.6 and 1.0 percent and industrial exports by -.3 and 6.2 percent. An important factor in this relative stagnation of exports was a government policy directed toward reducing the size of Yugoslav clearing account balances. Exports to eastern Europe were virtually stagnant between 1965 and 1969. Moreover, a tight credit policy was introduced with the reform of 1965; real investment and employment declined during 1965-1967. Export financing was affected by the restrictive credit policy. The elimination of export subsidies doubtlessly contributed to the sluggish export growth that occurred during the first few years following the launching of the reform. The credit screws were tightened further in 1967 in an unsuccessful attempt to reverse the export slowdown that had set in. The recovery of exports followed the relaxation of the restrictive monetary and credit policy; meanwhile export premiums were brought back as an export policy tool.

In summary, the constant-market-shares analysis applied to the 1961-1965 and 1965-1972 periods provides evidence that increased competitiveness was an important factor in the growth of Yugoslav exports during 1961-1965. However, in the latter period competitiveness became a negative influence on export expansion. The process of adapting to the new economic conditions which resulted from the economic reform of 1965 contributed to the deterioration in competitiveness. Attempts to reduce clearing balances and a tight monetary policy which depressed economic activity and adversely affected export financing should not be lost sight of. In addition, the trade discrimination effects associated with European regional trade blocs were increasingly being felt[1]. The disappearance of inefficient enterprises, foreseen to take place following the economic reform, does not appear to have occurred, nor have anticipated effects of the economic reform on efficiency within enterprises reached expectations. Investment allocation following the shift from government investment funds may have become less rational. The law passed in 1967 to allow Yugoslav enterprises to enter into joint ventures with foreign firms can be seen as recognition that stronger effects to increase productive efficiency were needed.

3. Structural Change in Trade in Manufactured Products[2]

Industrial exports increased about thirteenfold from 1952 to 1972, while total exports rose by a factor of nine (Table 25). In 1952, 4.6 percent of industrial output was exported (Table 26), while in 1972 the share had reached 13.9 percent[3]. These developments suggest that the economy has become more outward-oriented. Indeed, 16 of the 20 industry branches exported a larger share of their output in in 1972 than in 1952[4]. Further evidence that the economy has become

---

[1] A trade agreement was negotiated with the EEC in 1970.

[2] The terms manufactured exports and industrial exports are used synonymously and, unless specified otherwise, are defined as exports of the industrial sector, which includes manufacturing, mining and energy production.

[3] In 1962 and 1965 the share of industrial output exported was 10.6 and 15.3 percent, respectively (conversion rate used for export valuation was 750 old dinars per U.S. dollar in 1962 and 12.50 new dinars per dollar in 1965). When the three energy branches (electrical energy, coal and petroleum) are removed from the totals, the export/output ratios become 5.2 percent in 1952 and 19.8 percent in 1972.

[4] Changes in the export/output ratio must be interpreted with caution. The foreign exchange conversion rate used in the valuation of exports in domestic currency is extremely important here. This is especially so in

Table 25 - Value and Structure of Yugoslav Exports, 1952, 1962, 1972

	1952			1962			1972		
	value	total structure	industry structure	value	total structure	industry structure	value	total structure	industry structure
	mill. US $	percent		mill. US $	percent		mill. US $	percent	
Total exports	246.5	100		690.5	100		2,237.2	100	
Industry total	144.6	58.7	100	545.3	79.0	100	1,902.1	85.0	100
Electrical energy	.	.	.	1.2	.2	.2	3.2	.1	.2
Coal and coke	1.9	.8	1.3	1.3	.2	.2	5.5	.2	.3
Crude petroleum	2.0	.8	1.4	15.4	2.2	2.8	9.5	.4	.5
Ferrous metals	2.9	1.2	2.0	27.2	4.0	5.0	54.9	2.5	2.9
Non-ferrous metals	58.0	23.5	40.1	63.2	9.1	11.6	272.0	12.2	14.3
Non-metallic minerals	6.4	2.6	4.4	19.1	2.8	3.5	40.8	1.8	2.1
Metal products	.8	.3	.6	90.7	13.2	16.6	321.4	14.4	16.9
Shipbuilding	.	.	.	66.1	9.5	12.1	161.9	7.2	8.5
Electrical machinery, etc.	.1	.0	.1	29.3	4.2	5.4	168.2	7.5	8.8
Chemicals	6.9	2.8	4.8	17.0	2.4	3.1	162.4	7.3	8.5
Building materials	.1	.0	.1	1.2	.4	.2	2.5	.1	.1
Wood products	36.1	14.7	25.0	76.7	11.1	14.1	174.3	7.8	9.2
Paper and paper products	2.6	1.0	1.8	8.8	1.3	1.6	44.1	2.0	2.3
Textiles	3.7	1.5	2.6	40.8	6.0	7.5	224.1	10.0	11.8
Leather and footwear	1.6	.7	1.1	17.4	2.5	3.2	138.4	6.2	7.3
Rubber products	.0[a]	.0	.0	.9	.1	.2	13.6	.6	.7
Food products	12.8	5.2	8.8	47.9	7.0	8.8	65.1	2.9	3.4
Printing and publishing	.1	.0	.1	.3	.0	.0	6.8	.3	.4
Tobacco manufactures	8.6	3.5	5.9	20.4	3.0	3.7	33.3	1.5	1.8
Motion pictures	.0[b]	.0	.0	.5	.0	.1	.2	.0	.0
Agriculture, total	89.0	36.2	.	129.5	19.0	.	301.7	13.5	.
Vegetables and cereals	61.3	24.9	.	17.1	2.5	.	24.8	1.1	.
Fruits	2.3	1.0	.	8.2	1.2	.	8.4	.4	.
Livestock	24.1	9.8	.	84.0	12.2	.	226.6	10.2	.
Fisheries	1.4	.5	.	1.8	.3	.	3.1	.1	.
Home-processed agricultural products	.	.	.	18.5	2.8	.	38.9	1.7	.
Forestry	12.9	5.2	.	15.7	2.0	.	33.5	1.5	.

[a].011. - [b].005.

Source: Calculated from data in: SZzS [Statistički godišnjak SFRJ 1954, 1973]. - SZzS [Statistika spoljne trgovine SFRJ 1961, 1972].

---

the case of Yugoslavia since 1952; in the intervening years, the dinar/U.S. dollar official exchange rate has ranged from 300 old dinars (= 3 new dinars) to more than 17 new dinars per dollar (cf. Chapter III). That the Yugoslav official and/or settlement rate during most, if not all, of this period was not an equilibrium rate is a widely-held view. The equilibrium exchange rate is an elusive concept. One might think of it as that rate of exchange which is consistent with long-run balance of payments equilibrium under acceptable domestic conditions. The difficulty of taking proper account of price movements is also a hazard encountered in comparing export/output ratios over time. This problem is accentuated when a

Table 26 - Export/Output Ratios[a], 1952, 1972

	Export/output (percent)		Index of export/output	
	1952	1972	1952 = 100	1972 total industry = 100
Electrical energy	-	.5	56[b]	3
Coal and coke	1.2	1.7	142	12
Crude petroleum	2.7	2.0	74	14
Ferrous metals	1.7	8.6	506	62
Non-ferrous metals	31.4	27.9	89	201
Non-metallic minerals	6.3	18.8	298	135
Metal products	.2	14.2	7,100	102
Shipbuilding	-	54.5	160[c]	392
Electrical machinery, etc.	.1	19.4	19,400	140
Chemicals	5.0	15.3	306	110
Building materials	.1	.7	700	5
Wood products	13.0	20.7	159	149
Paper and paper products	3.8	15.1	397	109
Textiles	.5	15.5	3,100	112
Leather and footwear	1.6	34.1	2,131	245
Rubber products	.03	6.5	21,667	47
Food products	6.8	4.0	59	29
Printing and publishing	.2	1.8	900	13
Tobacco manufactures	5.4	12.8	237	92
Motion pictures	.3	1.5	500	11
Total industry	4.6	13.9	302	100

[a]Exchange rates used: 1952: 300 old dinars = 1 US $, 1972: 17 new dinars = 1 US $. - [b]1954 = 100. - [c]1956 = 100.

Source: SZzS [Statistički godišnjak SFRJ 1954, 1973].

large share of prices are government controlled, as they are in Yugoslavia. Adjusting the official exchange rate for price changes may mitigate the price problem somewhat. Adjusting the Yugoslav exchange rate by multiplying it by the ratio of the U.S. wholesale price index to the index of producers' prices of manufactured goods (1966 = 100) yields a "real", or purchasing-power-parity, exchange rate of 3.87 new dinars per U.S. dollar in 1952 and 13.60 in 1972. Using this "real" exchange rate as the conversion factor, the export/output ratio becomes 5.9, 13.5,

from the previously cited greater growth rate of exports in relation to the growth of production (Chapter IV). An important question concerning the export expansion that has taken place is: Have changes in the structure of exports been reflective of the nation's comparative advantage?

a. Capital and Labor Requirements and the Structure of Foreign Trade

In this section the familiar two-factor Heckscher-Ohlin model with its usual assumptions is used to test whether Yugoslavia's foreign trade reflects the country's comparative advantage[1]. Comparative advantage is defined in terms of relative endowments of capital and labor. The assumption is made that labor is relatively abundant in Yugoslavia. Support for this assumption is provided by the large net outflow of Yugoslav workers to the factories of western Europe (and to a much smaller extent to eastern Europe) that has taken place since the mid-1960s (cf. Chapter IV) and the net capital inflow that has been experienced. Capital flows from the United States during 1949-1961 (the U.S. was the dominant supplier of capital during this period) averaged US $ 155 million per year[2]. The annual total net inflow of medium and long-term capital averaged about US $ 200 million during 1961-1972.

Vectors of direct capital- and labor-output ratios were multiplied by the Leontief inverse matrix, $(I - A)^{-1}$, to yield total capital- and la-

---

16.4 and 11.1 percent in 1952, 1962, 1965 and 1972, respectively. The decline in the ratio in 1972 indicates that changes in the nominal exchange rate since 1965 did not keep pace with the relatively high rate of inflation in Yugoslavia. Another problem involved in a comparison of the foreign trade ratio over time is that Yugoslavia has employed multiple exchange rates to a considerable extent, as well as export subsidies. If not taken into account, these constitute additional distorting factors.

[1] For the original formulation of the Heckscher-Ohlin model see Heckscher [1949]. - Ohlin [1967]. - Empirical tests of the Heckscher-Ohlin model have yielded mixed results. Consequently, attempts to find alternative explanations of trade structure have been made. Alternative theories that have been advocated focus on heterogeneous factors and products, technology, factor intensity reversals and demand conditions. For a good discussion of these alternative explanations of trade patterns see Ellsworth, Leith [1975, Chapters 7 and 8]. - Baldwin [1971].

[2] World Bank [1975, p. 289]. See Chapter 13 of this Country Economic Report for a discussion of capital flows and external debt.

bor-output ratios for 29 economic sectors in 1968 (Table A 14)[1]. These ratios were multiplied by the exports (imports) of each respective sector to produce the total capital and labor requirements of the exports (imports) of each sector. By summing these sectoral factor requirements the total capital and labor requirements of exports and imports are obtained (Table A 15).

The ratios of capital/labor requirements of various groups of exports and imports are presented in Table 27. Looking at the bottom two rows of the Table it is seen that the capital-intensity of total exports exceeds that of total imports. For a relatively capital-scarce country

Table 27 - Capital and Labor Embodied in Yugoslav Industrial Exports and Imports, 1968

Trade	Capital	Labor	C/L
	10, 000 new dinars	tens of man-years	
Exports[a]	2,378,527.9	715,139.2	3.33
Imports[a]	3,441,045.1	941,768.5	3.65
Exports[b]	1,237,947.7	428,036.2	2.89
Imports[b]	2,747,911.1	739,945.9	3.71
Exports[c]	971,530.1	230,520.3	4.21
Imports[c]	2,701,544.5	621,878.3	4.34
Exports[d]	3,683,401.4	1,317,252.4	2.80
Imports[d]	3,846,484.4	1,430,958.7	2.69

[a]Sectors 4-21 of Table A 15. - [b]Sectors 4, 7-10, 14, 15 of Table A 15. - [c]Sectors 3, 4, 7-10 of Table A 15. - [d]All sectors of Table A 15.

Source: Table A 15.

[1] This methodology owes its origin to Wassily Leontief's pioneering work "Domestic Production and Foreign Trade: The American Capital Position Re-examined" [1953].

this is not what would be expected. However, included in total trade are non-competitive imports, i.e., imports of goods whose domestic elasticity of supply is extremely low, e.g., coffee, tea and cocoa, and commodities whose production location is tied to an input source, i.e., supply-oriented industries such as mineral production. In relating foreign trade structure to capital and labor endowments it is more meaningful to look at certain sub-categories of exports and imports. The first two rows of Table 27 relate to trade in sectors 4-21 of Table A 15, i.e., industrial sector (Yugoslav definition) goods minus electrical energy, coal and crude petroleum production and processing. Here the "right" relationship between the export and import capital/ labor ratios appears; the capital intensity of imports is 9.6 percent greater than that of exports.

In addition, the factor requirements of two other export and import groups have been calculated. First, industrial sector exports and imports were reduced by attempting to exclude goods for which the nation's natural endowment is a major determinant of comparative advantage, i.e., domestic (non-capital and -labor) resource-related industries. After this process of elimination the remaining industries consist of ferrous metals, metal products, shipbuilding, electrical machinery, chemicals, textiles, and leather and footwear. This time the capital-intensity of imports is greater than that of exports by a substantial 28.4 percent. The most exclusive group of commodities includes six newly-created industries (petroleum, ferrous metallurgy, metal products, shipbuilding, electrical machinery and chemicals). These industries were established mainly during the period of central planning and were favored by the export coefficient and subsidy system that existed from 1952 to 1965. Again the ratios have the "correct" relationship; the capital-intensity of imports exceeds that of exports by 3.1 percent. The capital-intensity of this latter import group vis-à-vis the capital-intensity of exports is relatively low, implying that Yugoslavia has a greater comparative advantage in the more traditional products such as textiles (including clothing) and leather and footwear. This is not at all surprising. Nevertheless, based on the simple two-factor model, Yugoslav industrial trade is consistent with the nation's labor and capital endowment[1].

---

[1] This does not imply that the nation's foreign trade structure is optimal, as will become evident in following sections.

b. Comparative Advantage and Net Export and Import Industries

In this section the assumption that labor is homogeneous is relaxed; two categories of labor, skilled and unskilled, are considered[1]. It is assumed that, as between physical capital, skilled and unskilled labor, Yugoslavia's relatively abundant factor is unskilled labor[2]. Support for this assumption is derived from the fact that an estimated 3 percent of the total labor force has near zero marginal productivity and about 70 percent are unskilled in the sense that the highest level of education attained does not exceed the level of primary school[3].

The assumption that unskilled labor is relatively abundant in Yugoslavia leads to the hypothesis that the country has a comparative advantage in products using relatively much of unskilled labor and relatively little of physical capital and skilled labor[4]. The next step in the analysis is to classify the various industrial branches according to their capital-labor, skilled-unskilled labor intensities. For this calculation, the cumulative, i.e., direct plus indirect, capital/labor ratios have been used to rank the industry branches according to their capital (or labor) intensities (Table A 14)[5]. Additionally the industries have been classified as being relatively skilled or unskilled labor-intensive. In making this classification, use has been made of both the wage value-added per employee and the ratio of personnel with secondary education and above, highly skilled and skilled workers to total employees (Table A 16)[6]. Finally, each of the twenty industrial branches was put into one of the following categories: capital and skilled labor-intensive, capital and unskilled labor-intensive, labor and skilled labor-intensive, and labor and unskilled labor-intensive (Table 28).

---

[1] On attempts to link comparative advantage to labor of different types see Keesing [1965, 1966]. - See also Lary [1968].

[2] There are regions, however, where a scarcity of unskilled labor exists, e.g., in Slovenia.

[3] Kayser [1972, p. 30]. - SZzS [Statistički godišnjak SFRJ 1974, pp. 105, 109].

[4] However, see the reference to comparative advantage in Chapter I.

[5] Industry branches with a capital/labor ratio above the average for all of industry have been classified as being capital-intensive.

[6] An industry is classified as skilled labor-intensive if the value of the indicator for that industry exceeds the average for all of industry, with adjustments being made for discrepancies between the two indicators, wage value-added per employee and the ratio of personnel with secondary education and above, highly skilled and skilled workers to total employees. See Lary [1968] for an application of wage value-added in the analysis of trade patterns.

Table 28 - Classification of Industries According to Capital-Labor and Skilled-Unskilled Labor Intensity, 1968

Classification	Industries
1. Capital and skilled labor-intensive	electrical energy, petroleum, ferrous metals, non-ferrous metals, chemicals
2. Capital and unskilled labor-intensive	paper and paper products
3. Labor and skilled labor-intensive	printing, shipbuilding, motion pictures, electrical machinery, etc., metal products
4. Labor and unskilled labor-intensive	wood products[a], coal, building materials, non-metallic minerals, rubber products, food products, textiles, leather and footwear, tobacco manufactures

[a]Wood products are classified as being labor-intensive, contrary to the data in Table A 14. Although the fixed capital in this industry was checked in various sources for accuracy, the fixed capital figure in Table A 14 appears vastly overstated when compared with its value in other years. Using 1969 data, the wood products industry ranks 12th in terms of the direct capital/output ratio and 19th in terms of the direct capital/labor ratio.

Source: Tables A 14 and A 16.

This classification of industries according to factor-intensity serves as a frame of reference for analyzing the structure of trade in manufactured goods in 1968. In this analysis the industrial branches are classified as net exporters or net importers (Table 29). It is not uncommon for a country to export and import the same product. At the two-digit level of industrial classification most countries both export and import goods in the same product classification. Based on the assumption that Yugoslavia's relative abundant factor is unskilled labor, it is hypothesized that unskilled labor-intensive industries will be net exporters and capital and skilled labor-intensive industries will have a net import balance.

Table 29 - Net Exports and Imports and Factor Intensiveness[a], 1968 (ranking)

	1,000 new dinars	K*/L*	L/X	L*/X	K/X	K*/X	Personnel with secondary and above education, skilled and highly skilled - total employed	Wage value-added per employee
Net exporters								
Wood products[b]	1,291,203	6	2	15	4	2	18	19
Shipbuilding	1,130,879	10	14	14	13	10	4	5
Leather and footwear	705,207	19	8	3	20	19	11	17
Non-ferrous metals	638,070	5	13	13	6	5	9	6
Tobacco manufactures	306,515	20	17	1	18	15	16	12
Textiles	88,633	18	5	4	12	16	19	20
Paper and paper products	52,558	2	11	7	2	1	15	15
Motion pictures	5,539	11	19	20	19	20	1	1
Net importers								
Metal products	7,067,215	13	7	9	11	9	5	11
Chemicals	1,996,059	7	15	16	10	7	10	7
Ferrous metals	1,212,340	4	12	6	5	3	6	9
Crude petroleum	977,981	3	20	18	7	8	3	2
Electrical machinery, etc.	601,322	12	16	12	17	11	8	8
Rubber products	333,348	16	6	11	16	18	12	14
Coal and coke	326,585	8	1	10	3	6	13	16
Non-metallic minerals	243,919	15	3	8	8	12	17	18
Printing, etc.	72,407	9	9	17	15	13	7	3
Electrical energy	34,988	1	18	19	1	4	2	4
Building materials	19,323	14	4	15	9	14	20	13
Food products	4,876	17	16	2	14	17	14	10

[a] K is direct capital, K* cumulative (direct and indirect) capital, L is labor, L* cumulative labor (in physical units). - [b] See footnote, Table 28.

Source: Tables A 14, A 16. - SZzS [Medjusobni adnosi privrednih delatnosti SFRJ 1968].

Of the net export group in 1968, only non-ferrous metals and the paper industry have cumulative capital/labor ratios that exceed the industrial average. The appearance of these two industries in the net export group can be explained, however, on the basis of their usage of natural resources, with which Yugoslavia is relatively well-endowed. Yugoslavia is the leading European producer of antimony, chrome, copper, lead and molybdenum; she is Europe's second largest producer of mercury, with about 10 percent of the world output of this product, and is a major producer of bauxite and zinc. Vast amounts of timber are also found in Yugoslavia. With the exception of non-ferrous metals, shipbuilding and the motion picture industry, the net exporters also tend to use relatively much unskilled labor in their production. Of these three, the motion picture industry is a special case while the position of the other two as net exporters can be explained by looking at nature's benevolence to the country.

The position of rubber products, coal, non-metals, building materials and food manufactures is contrary to expectations based on factor endowments. As previously explained, government price and investment policies have hindered the development of the primary and semi-manufactured goods industries[1]. This strategy of giving preference to industries producing finished and highly-processed goods has contributed to a somewhat "top-heavy" structure of the economy and thus a trade pattern that is somewhat out of line with expectations based on the nation's comparative advantage. It should be kept in mind, however, that a country's foreign trade structure reflects not only domestic policies and conditions but economic policies in the rest of the world as well[2].

c. Hypothetical and "Revealed" Comparative Advantage

In this section changes in the structure of trade in manufactured goods are examined in order to determine if the pattern of trade has moved closer to expectations based on comparative advantage. A hypothesized structure of comparative advantage is compared to the pattern of "revealed" comparative advantage. "Revealed" comparative advantage is defined in terms of the ratio: $E_i - M_i/E_i + M_i$, where E_i and M_i are the value of exports and imports, respectively, of industry branch i. Higher values of this ratio are assumed to be indicative of greater comparative advantage than lower values[3].

In order to compare the structure of the "revealed" with that of the hypothesized comparative advantage, the twenty industrial branches are ranked according to comparative advantage by calculating the sum of each branch's ranking according to cumulative capital-labor intensity (increasing order) and skill intensity (increasing order) and then ranking the branches according to this rank sum; comparative advantage decreases with increases in the sum total. While this method of estimating the structure of comparative advantage ignores problems

---

[1] See also Nikolin [1973]. Nikolin states that the production of industrial materials began to lag behind the requirements of domestic enterprises on a major scale in about 1960. He cites power, steel, non-ferrous metals, cement and building materials als being in continual short supply; shortages of chemical semi-manufactures, primary wood products, and raw material inputs of the footwear, rubber, paper and textile industries tend to be more irregular [p. 61].

[2] For an analysis of the effects of protection on foreign trade patterns, see Travis [1964].

[3] The technique used here is similar to the one used by Balassa [1965].

of aggregation and the influences of productive factors other than capital and labor, it does make possible a preliminary quantitative, as opposed to a qualitative, comparison of "revealed" and hypothetical structures of comparative advantage.

The ranking of industries on the basis of "revealed" and hypothetical comparative advantage is presented in Table 30. Certain industries in which Yugoslavia's natural resource endowment plays a major role are subject to a downward bias in the hypothetical ranking. In spite of this, it was decided not to incorporate qualitative judgements into the structure of hypothetical comparative advantage. The Spearman

Table 30 - Hypothetical and "Revealed" Comparative Advantage, 1952, 1962, 1972

	$\frac{E_i - M_i}{E_i + M_i}$			Ranking			Ranking of hypothetical comparative advantage
	1952	1962	1972	1952	1962	1972	
Electrical energy	-	1.000	.577	-	1	5	20
Coal and coke	-.808	-.903	-.812	12	19	18	10
Crude petroleum	-.709	-.223	-.861	11	13	20	19
Ferrous metals	-.809	-.501	-.649	13	16	17	18
Non-ferrous metals	.857	.478	.134	3	7	6	15.5
Non-metallic minerals	-.137	.172	-.360	5	8	11	4
Metal products	-.985	-.499	-.518	16	15	15	11
Shipbuilding	-	.736	.836	-	5	1	15.5
Electrical machinery, etc.	-.994	-.181	.005	17	12	7	9
Chemicals	-.428	-.662	-.445	8	17	13	12.5
Building materials	.619	.955	-.389	4	2	12	3
Wood products	.973	.936	.617	2	3	3	8
Paper and paper products	-.257	.089	-.016	6	9	8	12.5
Textiles	-.858	-.434	-.045	14	14	9	1
Leather and footwear	-.449	.946	.588	9	4	4	6
Rubber products	-.997	-.904	-.599	18	20	16	7
Food products	-.314	.043	-.451	7	11	14	5
Printing and publishing	-.623	-.766	-.169	10	18	10	14
Tobacco manufactures	1.000	.704	.722	1	6	2	2
Motion pictures	-.953	-.060	-.833	15	10	19	17

Source: SZzS [Statistika spoljne trgovine SFRJ, various years]. - Tables A 14, A 16.

rank correlation coefficient was used to compare the "revealed" with the hypothetical structure. The magnitude of this coefficient for 1952, 1962 and 1972 is .253, -.001 and .220 respectively.

Thus the "revealed" structure of comparative advantage is not very similar to the hypothesized structure. The structures became more dissimilar during the first decade of workers' management, followed by a closer correspondence during the period of the major foreign trade reforms. This suggests that foreign trade policy was somewhat more rational during the second decade of workers' self-management than during the first. However, these results should be treated with caution. It has been implicitly assumed that the hypothetical structure of comparative advantage did not change over time. Factors other than capital and labor have not been considered. And any given nation's pattern of foreign trade is influenced by the commercial policies of other countries.

d. Contribution of Industrial Branches to Incremental Industrial Exports

In this section the contribution of the various industrial branches to the growth of industrial exports in the pre-reform period of 1952-1961 is compared to that in the reform years of 1961-1972 (Table 31). The purpose of this investigation is to provide information on the effects of government policy on incremental export earnings and the efficiency of the industrial sector in earning foreign exchange[1].

The performance of the unskilled labor-intensive industries in the latter period as contrasted to the former is somewhat mixed. While the contribution of the entire group declined from 47.1 to 33.6 percent of incremental exports, this decrease was entirely accounted for by the fall in the importance of exports of food products. Exports of food products encountered severe growth problems in the 1960s. Although there was a growth spurt in the late 1960s, declines in the first two years of the 1970s resulted in 1972 exports being less than in 1965. Part of the export lag of this industry can be traced to production problems. Agricultural production in 1972 was only 4.5 percent greater than in 1961, while 1961 output was 92.6 percent greater than that of 1952[2].

---

[1] The contribution of a given industry branch to the growth of industrial exports is computed by dividing the change in exports of the branch by the change in total industrial exports.

[2] The price reform of 1965 in which producers' prices of agricultural goods rose by 43 percent, while producers' prices of industrial goods

Table 31 - Industrial Branch Contribution[a] to the Growth in Value of Industrial Exports[b], 1952-1961, 1961-1972 (percent)

	1952-1961	1961-1972
Electrical energy	.2	.2
Coal and coke	.1	.2
Crude petroleum	1.2	.3
Ferrous metals	6.4	2.3
Non-ferrous metals	-2.2	14.9
Non-metallic minerals	2.9	1.8
Metal products	23.8	17.2
Shipbuilding	9.9	9.1
Electrical machinery, etc.	9.0	9.6
Chemicals	2.9	10.0
Building materials	.4	.1
Wood products	10.5	7.4
Paper and paper products	1.3	2.6
Textiles	11.7	12.7
Leather and footwear	4.4	8.5
Rubber products	.1	.9
Food products	14.5	.8
Printing and publishing	.2	.4
Tobacco manufactures	2.5	1.2
Motion pictures	.2	-

[a]Contribution of branch i = $\frac{\Delta E_i}{\Delta \sum_i E_i}$ where E = export value. -

[b]Total industrial exports (mill. US $): 1952: 144.72, 1961: 424.80, 1972: 1,902.05.

Source: SZzS [Statistika spoljne trgovine SFRJ, various years].

rose by only 15 percent, was probably a contributing factor to the 16 percent increase in agricultural output that took place in 1966. Neither continuous high growth in output nor increases of this magnitude in the terms of trade of agriculture relative to industry followed this burst of output. Agricultural growth was negative in 1952, 1961 and 1972, although the decline was more severe in 1952 than in the other two years.

Largely influenced by the non-ferrous metals and chemical industries, the share of capital-skill-intensive exports in incremental manufactured exports during 1961-1972 was 3.26 times what it was during the earlier period. Exports of non-ferrous metals were on a downward trend during the 1950s and did not reach their 1952 level again until 1962. In the meantime their share of total industrial exports fell from over 40 to less than 12 percent. Since 1962, non-ferrous metals exports have grown faster than the industrial average (imports have grown even faster, see footnote 1, p. 90). The chemical industry, as its share of industrial investment rose from 6.4 percent in 1952-1960 to 8.2 percent in 1961-1971, moved from a lagging export growth sector to a leading one. This industry has been a major recipient of direct investment from abroad (cf. Chapter VI). The effects of foreign investment on exports have probably been slight up to now, however.

In this section the contribution of the various industry branches to the growth in the value of industrial exports before and after the major foreign trade reforms of the 1960s was examined. From this analysis no clear picture emerges regarding the effects of the economic reforms on incremental exchange earnings although there has been some tendency for the capital-intensive branches to provide a greater share of export earnings since the reforms.

4. Import Requirements and Net Total Exports

In the preceding sections exports and imports were defined in standard commodity composition terms. Exports of steel, for example, were defined to include exports of those articles coming under the general definition of steel; imports were treated in the same way. While this definitional concept has obvious advantages and uses, it also has certain limitations. In particular, this definition of exports and imports is inappropriate for analyzing the net balance of trade effects of the exports of the various industries. In this section the import content of production as well as the "net total exports" of the various industry branches will be calculated. The "net total exports" concept refers to the direct and indirect exports of each industry branch out of its value-added. In this way a more realistic picture of the export supply position is obtained.

It has become customary to examine imports of various products in direct terms and, for particular types of analysis, in total terms, where total refers to the sum of direct and indirect imports[1]. For example, the total imports, m_j^*, required for the production of one unit of good j can be computed as follows:

$$m_j^* = \sum_{i=1}^{n} m_i s_{ij}$$

where

$$m_i = \frac{\sum_i M_{ij}}{X_j}$$

X_j = value of production of good j

M_{ij} = value of direct imports used in the production of X_j, that is, the M_{ij}s are the import entries in the interindustry transactions table

s_{ij} = element of the $[I - A^{(D)}]^{-1}$ matrix

The total imports, M_j^*, used to produce various amounts of good j can then be found by simply multiplying m_j^* by the value of j production, e.g., X_j (Table 32).

The trend of the import content of production has been upward. Imported inputs as a share of output increased for 16 of 20 branches between 1962 and 1968. Between 1968 and 1970, 19 industry branches became more dependent on imported inputs[2]. All of the major economic groups in Table 33 have also become more import-dependent, especially between 1968 and 1970. Export production experiencend the sharpest rise in import requirements. Part of this trend to-

---

[1] Indirect imports of an industry consist of the import component of domestically purchased supplies. This concept of direct, indirect and total imports should not be confused with another notion of imports used, for example, to calculate the import/total supplies ratio (see Chapter IV). The latter deals with imports of specific goods; in this section the reference is to the imports used in producing specific goods. On the import requirements of production, see also Sekulić [1972].

[2] Import requirements in 1970 for 29 sectors are available from the author.

Table 32 - Yugoslav Import Requirements of Production and Exports, 1962, 1968

	$m_i = \sum_i \frac{M_{ij}}{X_i}$ = direct imports per unit of output		$m^*_j = \sum_i m_i s_{ij}$ = total imports per unit of output		$M^*_j = m^*_j E_j$ = total import requirement of exports		$E_j - m^*_j E_j$ = direct exports net of import requirements	
					1,000 new dinars			
	1962	1968	1962	1968	1962	1968	1962	1968
Electrical energy	.0080	.0206	.0585	.0566	742	288	11,948	3,968
Coal and coke	.1139	.1222	.1491	.1516	1,079	1,572	6,161	8,797
Crude petroleum, etc.	.1220	.2676	.1716	.3416	22,588	49,782	109,042	95,950
Ferrous metals	.0676	.0878	.1874	.2323	51,887	84,046	224,983	277,035
Non-ferrous metals	.0628	.1230	.1476	.2647	70,535	442,633	407,345	1,229,572
Non-metallic minerals	.0459	.0594	.0918	.1234	12,264	44,986	121,326	319,570
Metal products	.0922	.0885	.1601	.1798	164,563	360,356	808,607	1,643,828
Shipbuilding	.3063	.2400	.3742	.3087	245,861	481,035	411,169	1,077,225
Electrical machinery, etc.	.1165	.1144	.1964	.2232	64,541	260,064	264,079	905,098
Chemicals	.1641	.2070	.2273	.2976	50,649	325,770	172,180	768,886
Building materials	.0323	.0311	.0797	.0784	5,019	8,225	57,951	96,686
Wood products	.0156	.0654	.0591	.1205	37,411	173,011	595,609	1,262,761
Paper and paper products	.0323	.0760	.0764	.1601	6,065	66,561	73,315	349,187
Textiles	.1654	.1718	.2696	.2913	116,119	500,810	314,591	1,218,414
Leather and footwear	.1282	.1413	.2293	.2403	43,783	216,882	147,157	685,663
Rubber products	.2865	.2489	.3279	.3101	2,774	17,301	5,686	38,492
Food products	.0564	.0853	.0982	.1322	52,011	116,215	517,638	762,870
Printing and publishing	.0353	.0509	.0719	.1049	201	3,462	2,589	29,544
Tobacco manufactures	.0380	.0257	.0584	.0784	18,319	24,840	295,371	291,997
Motion pictures	.0343	.0553	.0811	.0925	1,824	1,403	20,666	13,766
Miscellaneous manufacturing	.0416	.0892	.1000	.1715	2,988	13,468	26,892	65,061
Agriculture	.0165	.0176	.0411	.0486	29,854	119,077	696,516	2,331,060
Forestry	.0037	.0058	.0151	.0194	1,334	3,904	78,016	197,316
Construction	.0092	.0137	.0605	.0707	230	19,904	3,570	261,616
Transport and communication	.0804	.1011	.1283	.1405	140,820	466,215	956,760	2,852,041
Trade and catering	.0028	.0032	.0160	.0138	8,251	29,874	507,459	2,128,381
Service rendering arts and crafts	.0396	.0401	.0962	.0973	-	2,770	-	25,695
Public utilities	.0091	.0198	.0416	.0498	-	-	-	-
Scrap and waste	-	-	-	-	-	-	10,080	50,762
Total					1,151,712	3,834,404	6,845,626	18,991,241

Source: Calculated from data in: SZzS [Medjusobni odnosi privrednih delatnosti SFRJ 1962, 1966, 1968].

Table 33 - Total Import Content of Major Sectoral Groups, 1962-1970 (percent)

Sector	1962	1966	1968	1970
Gross output	11.0	11.9	12.5	15.2
Investment	26.5	24.7	26.0	28.5
Industrial investment	57.8	59.1	63.0	66.2
Consumption - private and public	15.1	15.2	15.4	16.8
Total exports	14.5	15.3	16.8	21.5
Industrial exports	17.5	20.2	22.3	27.5

Source: Calculated from data in SZzS [Medjusobni odnosi privrednih delatnosti SFRJ 1962, 1966, 1968, 1970].

ward a greater reliance on imported inputs can be explained by business cycle conditions. The break in the trend in 1966 reflects the economic slump that had set in. The economy in 1968 began to move out of the recession that saw no growth of industrial production in 1967. By 1970 the economy was moving along with a good head of steam, as industrial production rose by 11 percent in 1969 and 9 percent in 1970. Other factors contributing to the increase in the use of imported inputs include import liberalization, the use of the foreign exchange retention quota as an export promotion instrument, the development strategy of promoting manufacturing industries at the expense of the primary sector, and dinar devaluation speculation (the dinar was devalued twice in 1971).

Among the most import-intensive industries are those whose growth has been of an import substituting type, for example, ferrous metals, metal products, electrical machinery, chemicals, rubber products and leather and footwear. Thus the effect of import substitution policies on the trade balance can be seen to be different than would be implied by the ratio of the imports of a particular commodity to the total domestic supplies of the same good. It can also be seen in Table 32 that the major export sectors, with the exception of wood, food and tobacco products, have a relatively high import content of production. The export retention quota, which permits firms to retain a certain share of their foreign exchange earnings, plays a role in this association between import intensity of production and export shares.

The total import concept is useful in analyzing the balance-of-payments effect of an industry's exports. Letting E_j refer to the value of exports of good j, the total imports, M_j^*, generated in the production of E_j are calculated as follows:

$$M_j^* = m_j^* \; E_j$$

Thus by examining not only the direct imports used in producing j, but also the imported component of the intermediate inputs used in the production process, one obtains a more complete picture of the way in which industry j, through its exports, affects the balance of payments.

This, however, is not the complete picture. Granted, the consideration of the import content of intermediate inputs provides more information on the net foreign exchange impact of industry j exports than merely comparing E_j with $m_i E_j$. But stopping at this point, an unnecessary asymmetric situation with respect to the treatment of exports (direct only) and imports (direct plus indirect) remains, as well as a degree of accuracy regarding the balance-of-payments effects of exports that is less than obtainable[1].

The measurement of the balance-of-payments effect of export can be improved by carrying the analysis one step further and considering indirect as well as direct exports. Suppose direct exports of steel (from foreign trade statistics) are equal to 100 currency units, and M_j^* (= $m_j^* E_j$) is 30. The balance-of-payments effect of steel exports is then equal to 70. But what about the amount of steel that is contained in exports of goods in which steel is used as an intermediate input? Ignoring the indirect exports of steel (in machinery and consumer durables, for example) results in an underestimation of the actual amount of steel exported. And by the same token, by including the indirect exports of other industries, for example, iron ore, the value of steel exports is overestimated.

[1] Symmetry between exports and imports is also discussed in Chittle [1974].

Net total (direct and indirect) exports (E_i^*) of industry i can be computed as follows:

$$E_i^* = \sum_i v_i s_{ij} E_j$$

where

E_i^* = total exports of industry i

E_j = a vector of direct exports

$v_i = \frac{V_i}{X_i}$ = proportion of value-added in the gross output of industry i

The proportional factor v_i serves to avoid overvaluation or double counting. Thus each element of the ith row of the $[I - A^{(D)}]^{-1}$ matrix is multiplied by v_i to yield the value-added of i necessary to produce one unit of each of the j commodities. The sum of the product of each element of the redefined row of s_{ij}s and the respective element of the E vector yields the net total exports of industry i[1]. A net total exports vector, E, is then defined as follows:

$$E^* = V\,[I - A^{(D)}]^{-1}\,E$$

where E^* is a vector of net total exports, V a diagonal matrix whose diagonal elements are the value-added/gross output ratios (v_is) of the various industries, and E is a vector of direct exports[2].

---

[1] It is assumed that the value-added proportion of gross output is uniform regardless of where the product is sold, for example, in the domestic or foreign markets.

[2] This method of calculating total exports has been used by Tuvia Blumenthal [1972] to calculate the total exports of various Japanese industries. Blumenthal used the total export figures to calculate the structure of exports and the export/output ratio; he did not apply the concept to balance-of-payments analysis. He also evidently did not have data on the specific M_{ij}s for the interindustry transactions matrix ("implicit is the assumption that the total imports, M_i, is the same per unit of output, whether used as an intermediate or final use" [p. 630]).

E_i^* is a measure of the value-added of industry i which is exported directly in the form of exports of the product(s) produced by industry i plus the value-added of industry i which is contained in the exports of each industry j which uses industry i output in its production process. Since E_i^* is a value-added measure, it is obviously net of imports. The balance-of-payments effect of the exports of industry i can then be seen by examining E_i^*, which is a more accurate measure than $E_i - M_j^*$.

A comparison of the definitions of E^* and E suggests certain hypotheses concerning the relative magnitudes of E^* and E for different economic sectors. E^* is hypothesized to be greater than E in those sectors which act mainly as suppliers of primary or intermediate inputs, since those sectors make a major contribution to export earnings by being embodied in the direct exports of other sectors. E^* is predicted to be less than E for those sectors producing mainly for final consumption.

Examples of the above relationships are not difficult to find in Table 34, where E^* has been calculated for 29 economic sectors in 1962 and 1968. Only a few will be cited here as illustrations. For example, the contribution of net total exports of the forestry sector to total export earnings of the economy on a value-added basis is about four times greater than the share of direct forestry exports in total direct exports, while the export share of the wood products industry on a value-added basis is considerably less than on a direct basis. The same type of relationship exists between the agriculture and food processing sectors. The shares of the energy sectors, electricity, coal and petroleum, in total manufactured exports on a value-added basis exceeds the shares of the same sectors in aggregate direct manufactured exports, while in the case of textiles, shipbuilding and leather and footwear the relationship is turned around. Especially pronounced is the reduction of shipbuilding exports when calculated on a net total exports basis. This industry has benefited much from export promotion policies.

The value-added measure of exports, in addition to providing information on the source of foreign exchange earnings by economic sector (as can be seen, the difference between E^* and $E - m^*E$ as a measure of exports net of imported components is vast for some sectors) is especially useful in overall economic planning and coordination. By examining the production process more deeply it goes beyond the facade of direct exports by commodity. Whereas with the concept of direct exports the entire value of the exports of commodity i is attributed to the industry in which the commodity undergoes its last stage of processing prior to export, the value-added measure takes into account the entire production process and allocates export value to the various sectors according to their value-added contribution to the exported commodity. As a consequence, it provides economic planners and policy-makers with additional information and more clearly indicates the sources of the nation's foreign exchange earnings.

5. Geographical Export Patterns

Yugoslavia's trade structure is diversified by country as well as commodity. In 1973 she exported goods to at least 116 different countries. Italy, the Soviet Union and the Federal Republic of Germany are the most important markets for Yugoslav goods. In 1973 these three countries received 16.3, 14.3 and 11.2 percent, respectively, of Yugoslav merchandise exports. The same three countries are the leading sources of Yugoslav imports with Germany providing 19.1, Italy 11.9 and the Soviet Union 9.0 percent of total imports in 1973.

Information on the geographical structure of Yugoslav exports contained in Table 35 reveals that about one-half of total merchandise exports goes to western industrialized countries, one third to eastern Europe and one-sixth to the developing countries. An economic blockade was imposed by the Soviet bloc nations in 1948. By 1950 Yugoslav trade with these nations had virtually disappeared. Economic relations thawed slightly in 1954, but it was not until 1956 that normal trade relations were resumed. Yugoslavia has had an observer status with COMECON since 1956; since 1964 she has had a special status which allows her to participate only in those COMECON projects which she finds desirable[1]. Among the developing countries, the People's Republic of China, Libya, India, Iran and Egypt provided the major export markets in 1973. None of these countries accounted for more than 1.6 percent of Yugoslavia's total exports. Although oscillations have occurred, the long-term structure of exports according to western industrialized, eastern European and developing countries has been rather stable.

Yugoslav enterprises find the eastern European market for manufactured goods easier to enter than the western European market. Competition is not as strong in eastern Europe and there are fewer marketing difficulties, e.g., quality, design and technical standards are less rigorous. Moreover, prices in eastern markets tend to be higher

---

[1] Yugoslavia is also a member of GATT, ECE, IMF, IBRD, is associated with the OECD, and has a trade agreement with the EEC.

Table 34 - Yugoslav Direct and Net Total Exports, 1962, 1968

Sector	Direct exports (E)		Cumulative exports $[I-A^{(D)}]^{-1}E$		Value-added/ gross output		Net total exports (E*) $V[I-A^{(D)}]^{-1}E$ Col. 3xCol. 5	Net total exports (E*) $V[I-A^{(D)}]^{-1}E$ Col. 4xCol. 6
	1962	1968	1962	1968	1962	1968	1962	1968
	values in 1,000 new dinars							
1. Electrical energy	12,690	4,206	212,379	536,718	.6367	.7286	135.222	391,053
2. Coal and coke	7,240	10,369	274,353	440,926	.5858	.6441	160,716	284,000
3. Crude petroleum, etc.	131,630	145,732	339,818	537,452	.5579	.4281	189,584	230,083
4. Ferrous metals	276,870	361,801	1,072,141	1,814,527	.1842	.1909	197,488	346,393
5. Non-ferrous metals	477,880	1,672,205	1,164,526	3,925,635	.3208	.2589	373,580	1,016,347
6. Non-metallic minerals	133,590	364,556	244,741	597,775	.5661	.5318	138,548	317,897
7. Metal products	973,170	2,004,184	1,675,799	3,868,706	.4156	.4054	696,462	1,568,393
8. Shipbuilding	657,030	1,558,260	697,818	1,630,180	.2783	.3529	194,203	575,291
9. Electrical machinery, etc.	328,620	1,165,163	524,266	1,636,425	.3744	.3408	196,285	557,694
10. Chemicals	222,830	1,094,656	504,020	2,124,623	.4164	.3648	209,874	775,062
11. Building materials	62,970	104,911	110,265	229,437	.5620	.6051	61,969	138,832
12. Wood products	633,020	1,435,772	899,500	1,979,772	.3917	.3832	352,334	758,649
13. Paper and paper products	79,380	415,748	253,147	961,093	.4046	.2618	102,423	251,614
14. Textiles	430,710	1,719,224	737,179	2,851,638	.3605	.3331	265,753	949,881
15. Leather and footwear	190,940	902,545	275,817	1,238,389	.2952	.3097	81,421	382,291
16. Rubber products	8,460	55,793	68,242	209,080	.4792	.4573	32,702	95,612
17. Food products	529,650	879,085	597,913	1,068,618	.3468	.3054	207,356	326,357
18. Printing, etc.	2,790	33,006	37,227	99,054	.5873	.5616	21,863	56,619
19. Tobacco manufactures	313,690	316,837	360,907	416,609	.6339	.2734	228,779	113,901
20. Motion pictures	22,490	15,169	28,849	21,124	.5426	.5778	15,653	12,205
21. Miscellaneous manufacturing	29,880	78,529	33,515	81,825	.5136	.4198	17,213	34,350
22. Agriculture	726,370	2,450,137	1,631,444	4,648,418	.5462	.5625	891,095	2,614,735
23. Forestry	88,350	201,220	335,881	756,634	.8780	.8559	294,904	647,603
24. Construction	3,800	281,524	163,681	525,629	.4586	.4618	75,064	242,735
25. Transport and communication	1,097,580	3,318,256	1,459,239	4,172,485	.5937	.6444	866,350	2,688,749
26. Trade and catering	515,710	2,158,255	744,764	3,447,740	.8657	.9059	644,742	3,123,308
27. Service rendering arts and crafts	-	28,465	135,371	435,651	.5634	.5446	76,268	237,256
28. Public utilities	-	-	20,462	82,527	.6951	.7497	14,223	61,870
29. Scrap and waste	10,080	50,762	66,212	190,995	1.0000	1.0000	66,212	190,995
Total	7,967,420	22,826,369					6,808,286	18,989,755

Source: See Table 32. - For method of calculation see text.

Structure of exports (Sectors 1-29)				Structure of industrial exports (Sectors 1-20)			
net total exports	direct exports	net total exports	direct exports	net total exports	direct exports	net total exports	direct exports
1962	1962	1968	1968	1962	1962	1968	1968
percent							
2.0	.2	2.1	-	3.5	.2	4.3	-
2.4	.1	1.5	.1	4.2	.2	3.1	.1
2.8	1.7	1.3	.6	4.9	2.8	2.5	1.1
2.9	3.5	1.8	1.6	5.1	5.0	3.8	2.7
5.5	6.0	5.4	7.3	9.7	11.6	11.1	14.0
2.0	1.7	1.7	1.6	3.6	3.5	3.5	3.1
10.2	12.2	8.3	8.8	18.0	16.6	17.1	14.7
2.9	8.2	3.0	6.8	5.0	12.1	6.3	7.8
2.9	4.1	2.9	5.1	5.1	5.4	6.1	8.1
3.1	2.8	4.1	4.8	5.4	3.1	8.5	6.8
.9	.8	.7	.5	1.6	.2	1.5	.2
5.2	7.9	4.0	6.3	9.1	14.1	8.3	10.4
1.5	1.0	1.3	1.8	2.7	1.6	2.8	3.2
3.9	5.4	5.0	7.5	6.9	7.5	10.4	12.5
1.2	2.4	2.0	4.0	2.1	3.2	4.2	6.8
.5	.1	.5	.2	.8	.2	1.0	.4
3.0	6.6	1.7	3.9	5.4	8.8	3.6	5.4
.3	.1	.3	.1	.6	-	.6	.3
3.4	3.9	.6	1.4	5.9	3.7	1.2	2.4
.2	.3	.1	.1	.4	.1	.1	-
.3	.4	.2	.3				
13.1	9.1	13.8	10.7				
4.3	1.1	3.4	.9				
1.1	.1	1.3	1.2				
12.7	13.8	14.2	14.5				
9.5	6.4	16.5	9.5				
1.1	-	1.3	.1				
.2	-	-	-				
1.0	.1	-	.2				
100	100	100	100	100	100	100	100

Table 35 - Geographical Structure of Yugoslav Exports, 1948-1973 (percent)

Year	Western Europe			Eastern Europe	United States	Latin America	Asia	Africa	Other
	total	EC	EFTA						
1948	40.2	19.4	20.0	51.6	2.7	.5	1.2	3.8	-
1952	77.4	45.3	28.9	-	14.7	1.8	3.1	3.0	-
1953	66.6	37.3	23.4	-	14.0	1.6	14.7	3.1	-
1954	68.6	41.0	23.2	1.4	9.5	4.4	13.8	2.2	.1
1955	59.6	35.3	19.1	11.0	10.8	7.0	9.1	2.3	.2
1956	57.9	34.8	17.4	20.3	8.5	3.5	7.4	2.1	.3
1957	51.7	32.0	16.0	26.6	8.5	.5	6.7	5.9	.1
1958	50.6	28.6	18.7	27.8	7.4	1.0	6.4	6.6	.2
1959	45.7	26.2	16.0	30.9	6.5	1.9	9.8	5.1	.1
1960	45.1	25.6	8.1	32.2	6.9	1.7	8.4	5.6	.1
1961	45.9	26.0	15.7	30.8	6.4	2.1	9.9	4.7	.2
1962	44.1	27.2	15.0	24.3	7.6	4.6	11.7	7.4	.3
1963	48.3	33.9	12.9	26.6	5.9	2.0	8.4	8.4	.4
1964	43.0	27.5	13.3	34.6	5.8	2.4	9.4	4.7	.2
1965	36.1	25.1	8.8	42.4	5.7	1.5	9.3	4.8	.2
1966	41.8	27.7	11.1	36.5	6.2	1.3	9.3	4.7	.2
1967	44.6	29.7	11.9	36.0	6.3	1.4	7.9	3.6	.2
1968	45.4	28.0	12.7	33.3	7.1	1.5	8.3	4.2	.2
1969	50.3	32.0	14.0	29.1	6.3	2.6	7.3	3.9	.5
1970	51.5	33.0	14.4	30.8	5.3	1.3	7.0	3.6	.5
1971	45.8	29.1	14.1	36.5	6.0	2.3	5.2	3.8	.4
1972	48.9	30.6	14.9	35.3	6.7	2.3	4.0	2.4	.4
1973	45.9	32.2	11.1	32.4	8.2	2.2	6.9	3.9	.5

Source: SZzS [Statistika spoljne trgovine SFRJ, various years].

than in western trade. For the same reasons, Yugoslav importers have a preference for buying from the West. Since the Yugoslav balance on service account with the East tends toward surplus, she is not very keen on having a positive merchandise trade balance with these countries, as this involves the building up of bilateral credit balances[1]. Consequently, since 1967 prior approval has been a prerequisite for exporting to the clearing area and certain conditions may be attached to the approval of such exports, e.g., the exporter may be required to import certain goods from the clearing area or to export a certain quantity outside the clearing area[2].

The exports of a given country to state trading partner countries have been found to be less stable than exports to countries that do not have a state trading system[3]. To see if this holds true for Yugoslavia an "instability index" of Yugoslav exports to eastern Europe and the EEC has been calculated. The index was computed for the period from 1956, the first year of normal economic relations with eastern Europe following the economic blockade, to 1973. Instability was measured by calculating the annual average percentage deviation from trend[4]. The value of the index is 13.329 for exports to eastern Europe and 8.849 for exports to the EEC, indicating that exports to eastern Europe were less stable than exports to the EEC during 1956-1973. These results are consistent with a previous study which found Yugoslav exports and imports with the COMECON countries to be less stable than with the convertible currency area[5]. A possible explanation could be that political relations with eastern Europe are less stable and that

---

[1] Table A 17 contains information on Yugoslavia's merchandise trade balance with the convertible currency and bilateral clearing areas.

[2] Madžić [1969, p. 110]. - Efforts have recently been made to settle trade balances with eastern European countries in convertible currency. This method of payment now exists with respect to Rumania, Hungary, Poland and Bulgaria.

[3] See, for example, Behrman [1959].

[4] This index was used by the UN [Handbook 1972] to calculate an index of export fluctuation for a large number of developed and developing countries as follows:

$$F = \frac{100}{n} \sum_{i=1}^{n} \frac{[X_i - \hat{X}_i]}{X_i}$$

where F = fluctuation index

X_i = value of exports at time i

$\hat{X}_i$ = corresponding trend value (exponential trend)

n = number of years covered

[5] Madžar [1968]. - On Yugoslavia's trade with eastern and western Europe see also Jovanović [1972]. - Pertot [1967].

this instability affects trade flows. Other possible explanatory factors include the composition of exports to the two regions according to income elasticities of demand and economic growth rates of the two areas.

The structure of Yugoslav exports (by SITC one-digit sections) to the EEC, COMECON (= eastern Europe) and the developing countries (Tables 36-38) provides information concerning the broad categories of goods exported to groups of countries at various levels of industrialization. The EEC nations are among the most highly industrialized in the world, the developing countries are at the low end of the industrialization totem pole, while the countries of COMECON occupy a somewhat intermediate position. Thus labor-intensive goods would be expected to weigh more heavily in exports to the EEC than to the other two groups. The proximity and the industrial orientation of eastern Europe provide opportunities for exports of heavy manufactured goods, and consumer goods, which would not be competitive in western markets. The political position of Yugoslavia as a leader of the non-aligned nations and her advanced stage of industrialization vis-à-vis these nations imply relatively favorable market conditions for Yugoslavia's more capital and skill-intensive goods.

Looking first at the share of manufactures (SITC 5-8) in Yugoslavia's total exports to the three country groups, it is not surprising to find, given the increase in the share of manufactures in total exports to the world that has taken place, that the proportion of manufactures in total exports to each group has exhibited a rising trend. The increase in the share of manufactures has been especially pronounced in exports to the EEC, although the share remains considerably lower than is the case with exports to COMECON and the developing countries. The share of manufactures (SITC 5-8) in total exports by region in 1972 (with the 1960 share in parenthesis) was: EEC: 54.4 (21.9), COMECON: 84.6 (65.0), and Developing Countries: 83.7 (74.6)[1]. Yugoslavia's success in exporting manufactures to eastern Europe may help to explain a characteristic of her industrialization in which export expansion has gone hand-in-hand with import substitution.

---

[1] Roughly one-third of exports to the EEC in 1972 consisted of food and live animals. Fresh or frozen meat, of which beef is a major component, accounted for over 10 percent of Yugoslavia's exports to the EEC in 1972. Thus the importance to Yugoslavia of the EEC's ban on beef imports in 1974 can be seen.

Table 36 - Structure of Yugoslav Exports to EEC[a], 1960-1972 (percent)

SITC Section	1960	1961	1962	1963	1964	1965	1966	1967	1968	1969	1970	1971	1972
0	45.2	43.2	37.4	44.5	41.4	40.8	39.0	45.7	32.0	31.4	26.1	26.8	31.0
1	5.1	4.9	2.2	1.9	2.6	2.2	1.7	1.7	1.9	1.7	1.4	1.9	1.0
2	26.7	29.3	28.6	23.9	22.9	20.2	15.9	14.3	18.3	16.6	15.8	14.7	12.9
3	.7	.7	2.7	.8	.6	.5	1.6	1.7	.6	.4	1.3	1.9	.4
4	-	-	.1	-	-	.1	.1	.5	.4	.5	.2	.2	.1
5	1.8	1.4	1.3	1.3	2.1	2.3	3.2	2.6	3.3	2.7	3.3	4.0	4.3
6	14.4	13.1	18.8	18.6	17.8	19.2	22.9	19.7	26.0	28.4	30.1	23.3	23.2
7	.4	.8	1.5	1.8	2.7	4.0	3.7	3.5	4.3	6.3	10.1	13.8	15.1
8	5.3	6.4	7.4	7.2	9.9	10.7	11.8	10.1	13.0	12.1	11.8	13.2	11.8
9	.1	.1	.1	-	-	-	-	.2	.1	-	-	-	.2

[a]EEC here refers to the original six members.

Source: OECD [Trade by Commodities, various years].

Table 37 - Structure of Yugoslav Exports to Eastern Europe[a], 1960-1972 (percent)

SITC Section	1960	1961	1962	1963	1964	1965	1966	1967	1968	1969	1970	1971	1972
0	15.9	12.1	10.6	12.1	14.2	11.6	6.5	4.5	4.0	5.0	6.4	5.8	4.2
1	5.8	5.1	7.8	10.8	10.5	6.6	5.5	5.9	6.4	5.2	7.2	6.1	4.8
2	12.4	11.4	12.0	10.9	10.5	6.2	5.6	6.2	6.8	6.0	5.7	5.6	5.9
3	.5	.5	.9	.9	.4	.3	.2	.2	.2	1.1	.6	.5	.5
4	.2	-	.1	-	-	-	-	.1	-	-	-	.2	-
5	6.0	5.4	5.4	6.0	7.1	6.8	7.7	8.6	9.6	10.9	9.5	11.1	11.1
6	27.2	25.2	25.0	22.7	21.7	20.3	20.2	21.4	20.7	25.9	26.8	28.0	28.7
7	24.2	33.6	32.6	23.6	19.2	34.3	40.0	32.8	33.8	28.4	29.2	25.8	23.0
8	7.6	6.7	5.7	12.9	16.5	13.8	14.3	20.4	18.5	17.5	14.9	17.1	21.8
9	-	-	.1	.1	-	-	-	.1	-	-	-	-	-

[a]Countries included are U.S.S.R., German Democratic Republic, Poland, Czechoslovakia, Hungary, Romania, Bulgaria and Albania.

Source: Cf. Table 36.

Table 38 - Structure of Yugoslav Exports to Developing Countries, 1960-1972 (percent)

SITC Section	1960	1961	1962	1963	1964	1965	1966	1967	1968	1969	1970	1971	1972
0	9.2	9.5	3.6	6.2	4.7	2.5	3.6	8.7	3.0	3.7	2.6	3.4	5.1
1	2.2	2.2	.9	1.5	.4	2.0	1.2	.9	.6	.6	.5	-	.1
2	11.9	10.4	5.3	4.5	5.9	4.6	5.3	5.5	6.6	5.7	5.7	5.6	10.6
3	.7	1.8	3.4	2.8	2.4	2.2	1.8	2.8	.8	.1	-	.6	.4
4	-	-	-	-	-	-	-	-	-	-	-	-	.1
5	4.3	4.7	4.1	3.9	3.5	6.4	6.3	7.5	4.9	5.1	5.7	8.4	4.5
6	35.2	34.3	26.1	22.4	33.1	31.3	30.5	30.4	30.7	31.0	29.2	27.4	25.6
7	34.2	33.9	53.4	56.1	47.2	47.0	49.2	41.5	51.0	52.2	53.1	52.0	50.2
8	.9	3.0	3.1	2.3	2.5	3.8	2.1	2.8	2.4	1.7	2.6	2.8	3.4
9	.2	.2	.2	.3	.2	.1	.1	.1	.1	.1	-	-	.2

Source: Cf. Table 36.

The relatively low share of machinery and transport equipment in exports to the EEC is consistent with expectations based on Yugoslavia's comparative advantage vis-à-vis the various country groups. Within SITC 6, textile yarn and cotton fabrics are the most important products exported to the EEC, whereas ferrous and non-ferrous metals occupy the leading roles in exports to eastern Europe and the developing countries. The structure of Yugoslav exports by region in general is consistent with a priori expectations that the greatest scope for non-traditional exports is provided by the markets of eastern Europe and the developing countries. The developing countries may be the most dynamic market for Yugoslav exports in the near term. Yugoslavia has been making efforts to increase the share of her exports to developing countries for some years without much success. However, the share recently has been rising and in 1971 stood at 17 percent. Yugoslavia's friendly relations with some of the oil producing countries may be a plus factor concerning future growth of her exports to the Third World, as plans for rapid industrialization are beginning to be implemented.

6. Export Supply Factors

The constant-market-shares model used earlier in this chapter to identify the sources of export growth focuses mainly on demand considerations. In this section consideration is given to the supply side of the export picture. The purpose of this analysis is to bring into view the importance of certain supply variables in the movement of manufactured exports over time.

A simple single equation export supply model serves as the basis of analysis. A crucial assumption made is that the demand for Yugoslav exports is perfectly elastic. This assumption is not too implausible considering that Yugoslav exports constitute little more than one half of one percent of world exports[1]. The following export supply function is posited:

$$\ln E_t = a + b \ln R_t + c \ln I_t + d \ln C_t + e$$

where

E = real manufactured exports in U.S. dollars
R = "real" exchange rate

[1] The Yugoslav share of world exports of certain products is obviously much greater. The diversified structure of Yugoslav exports suggests that extremes in export shares are relatively few.

I = index of industrial production
C = chain index of industrial production
t = time in years
e = error term

The variable R, calculated by multiplying the official exchange rate by the ratio of world manufactured export prices to Yugoslav producers' prices, is inserted to examine the response of exports to changes in relative prices. The coefficient of R is hypothesized as being positive: Dinar devaluation or a relative rise in world prices acts as a stimulant to manufactured export growth. The effects of increased productivity and competitiveness associated with production taking place on a greater scale, that is, shifts in the export supply curve, are accounted for by the industrial production variable I. The chain index of industrial production is added to test the "recession-boom" effect[1]. A negative coefficient of C would indicate that manufactured export growth expands during a recession, as producers seek foreign markets to replace lost domestic sales; during a boom the incentive to export declines, as domestic sales become more attractive[2]. The equation, estimated for the period 1952-1972, yields the following result (with t-values in parentheses):

$$\ln E_t = \underset{(1.355)}{1.788} - \underset{(-1.583)}{.178} \ln R_t + \underset{(24.713)}{1.235} \ln I_t - \underset{(-1.770)}{.485} \ln C_t$$

$R^2 = .994$ D.W. = 2.235

The coefficient of I in the above equation provides evidence that for given values of R and C, an increase in industrial production of 10 percent is associated with a 12 percent increase in real industrial exports[3]. The negative sign of the coefficient of C suggests that producers may indeed become more interested in foreign markets during periods of domestic economic slump. However, confidence in the value of this coefficient is limited as it is significant at only between the .05 and .10 levels. The negative coefficient of R appears puzzling

---

[1] The chain index measures the year-to-year growth rates of industrial production.

[2] The equation was also estimated using a capacity utilization variable, defined in terms of deviations from the trend of industrial production, in place of the chain index. However, the results were less satisfactory than in the version of the equation presented here.

[3] It is an unsettled argument as to whether the line of causation runs from industrial production to exports or vice versa.

on the surface. One would expect it to have a positive sign, as an increase in R should provide an incentive for exporters to increase the amount supplied (and buyers to increase their purchases). However, data limitations prevented the calculation of the effective exchange rate used in the determination of export proceeds in dinars, e.g., it was not possible to incorporate the effects of export coefficients, subsidies and premiums on export remuneration. This, together with the fact that the coefficient is significant at a level of only between .10 and .20, suggests that the equation provides little information regarding the effects of price on export supply[1].

---

[1] Without R, the equation becomes:

$$\ln E_t = \underset{(1.516)}{2.060} + \underset{(54.032)}{1.163} \ln I_t - \underset{(-1.785)}{.508} \ln C_t$$

$R^2 = .993$ D.W. = 2.133

Excluding both R and C, the equation is:

$$\ln E_t = \underset{(-2.771)}{-.357} + \underset{(52.092)}{1.169} \ln I_t$$

$R^2 = .993$ D.W. = 1.724

Chapter VI: Foreign Direct Investment and Manufactured Export Expansion[1]

With the enactment of legislation in 1967, Yugoslavia became the first eastern European country to open its doors to foreign direct investment[2]. Following the approval of the first joint-venture contract on April 3, 1968, a total of 97 joint-venture contracts, with a foreign capital of US $ 137 million, were registered, as of January 31, 1974[3]. The circumstances surrounding this investment are quite unique. Western multinational corporations have accounted for an overwhelming share of the investment that has taken place. The investment takes the form of a particular type of joint venture between foreign firms and domestic enterprises, which are owned by "society", managed by workers, and operate in a substantially market economy within a socialist system. One of the reasons for allowing foreign risk capital to flow into the economy was to provide a stimulus to the growth of manufactured exports. In this chapter the economic, legal and institutional background of the decision to attract foreign capital is examined. In addition, the motives of the foreign investor are investigated.

1. The Decision to Permit Foreign Direct Investment in the Yugoslav Economy

The decision to allow foreign direct investment in Yugoslavia in cooperation with domestic enterprises should be viewed in light of the major economic reforms of 1965-1967. Among the aims of the reforms were: a rationalization of the investment structure; improved resource allocation and capacity utilization; increased productivity through better marketing, management and more advanced technology; more rapid employment growth; and greater integration into the world economy on the basis of comparative advantage[4]. The reforms provided for an increase in the scope of enterprise decision-making, e.g.,

---

[1] Much of this chapter is drawn from my article, "Direct Foreign Investment in a Socialist Labor-Managed Economy - The Yugoslav Experience" [Chittle 1975a].

[2] The term foreign direct investment is used in a broad context to include investment in which the foreigner has contractual rights but no ownership in the traditional sense.

[3] Excluding eight approved and registered contracts which either never became operational or were terminated after a short period.

[4] The reforms were discussed in Chapter III.

administrative restrictions on the distribution of enterprise earnings between wages and investment were removed and enterprises were permitted to engage in joint investment projects with domestic and foreign firms. This increase in enterprise autonomy can be seen as an attempt to strengthen the self-management system and to stimulate enterprise efficiency.

Foreign direct investment was also viewed as a means of improving Yugoslavia's international competitiveness by improving the efficiency of industrial production. The transfer of technology through the purchase of licenses had proved disappointing; the issuance of licenses did not keep up with technological developments. Moreover, Yugoslav enterprises were in need of direct access to foreign managerial techniques, marketing skills and sales networks. Foreign investment could improve the current account balance by contributing to an expansion of exports, especially of manufactured goods, and a reduction in the reliance on imports as import-competing industries became more competitive vis-à-vis foreign production. The inflow of financial capital that would make up part of the foreign direct investment could also help to finance the current account deficit. Financing the deficit had become a problem, as the share of the deficit financed by official long-term capital and transfers fell to 14.43 percent during 1966-1969, after being 91.82, 65.56 and 103.10 percent during 1947-1956, 1957-1961 and 1952-1965, respectively [Kovač 1973, p. 9].

Rising unemployment may also have contributed to the decision to provide an opportunity for foreign firms to engage in joint ventures with Yugoslav enterprises. Registered unemployment in 1967 was 2.5 times the level of 1957[1]. In addition, the absorption of Yugoslav labor reserves via emigration began to accelerate in the 1960s[2]. While the migration of these workers helped to ease the unemployment situation, Yugoslav leaders were not altogether happy to have so many of their citizens outside the country. Bringing western capital to the workers was seen as an alternative method of employment creation.

---

[1] Registered unemployment totaled 116 thousand in 1957 and 292 thousand in 1967. Unemployment as a percentage of total paid employment plus registered unemployment was 4.6 and 7.0 percent in 1957 and 1967 respectively (see Table A 10).

[2] From 1954 to 1960 the number of emigrant workers rose from 3,000 to 18,000, an average increase of 2,500 per year. The total reached 220,000 in 1967; the average annual increase from 1960 to 1967 was 29,000 (see Chapter IV and Table A 11).

2. Legal Basis and Form of Foreign Direct Investment[1]

As previously mentioned, foreign direct investment was made possible by legislation enacted in 1967[2]. The legislation has since been modified, with major changes occurring in 1971 and 1973 (changes in the regulations are discussed in the next section). Foreign direct investment in Yugoslavia takes place in the form of joint ventures in which foreign participation in the joint venture's total assets must be less than 50 percent[3]. The investment of the foreigner may take place in one of three types of domestic partner organizations: an existing enterprise (organization of associated labor), an existing or newly created division of an enterprise, or in a newly created enterprise. Investment of foreign capital is permitted in sectors of the economy other than banking, insurance, domestic transport, trade, public utilities and other services (except scientific research work, where investment is permitted); investment in these areas requires special permission. Up to now the bulk of foreign investment has been in industry. Investment of the foreign partner may be in the form of fixed assets, primary and intermediate goods, financial capital, technology, know-how and services[4].

---

[1] For further information on the regulations and other considerations concerning foreign investment in Yugoslavia, see Sukijasović [1970, 1973a, 1973b]. - Radovanović [1968]. - OECD [Foreign Investment 1974].

[2] Amendments to the Basic Law on Enterprises, Amendments to the Law on the Assets of Business Organizations, Amendments to the Basic Law on Unified Chambers of Commerce and Business Cooperation in the Economy, Law on the Taxation of Earnings of Foreign Persons Investing Capital in Domestic Business Organizations for the Purpose of Joint Ventures, Law on the Reform of the Law on Interest Rates Charged on Fixed Assets of Business Organizations [Official Gazette, No. 31/67].

[3] The question as to whether the joint ventures should be termed contractual or equity is avoided here, as is the related question concerning the ownership of the foreign-invested assets. Miodrag Sukijasović, a Yugoslav legal expert on foreign investment legislation, concludes that the joint venture is a quasi venture containing elements of both the contractual and equity forms [Sukijasović 1973b, Part Two, Chapter 3]. - The less than 50 percent requirement may be waived in extreme circumstances; it has not been waived to date. Only the broad highlights of the foreign investment regulations are brought out here; for more specific information see the references in footnote 1 above.

[4] About 15 percent of foreign investment has been in the form of financial capital [Komunist, August 19, 1974].

The foreign investment regulations provide broad guidelines for the investing partners, leaving the details to be worked out by the partners and specified in the contract. A proposed joint venture will normally not be approved by the Federal Secretariat of the Economy unless it is shown that the joint venture will result in an increase in production, exports and productivity; that modern production and management techniques will be employed (preferably technology not available in Yugoslavia); and that scientific research will be fostered. No specific minimum quantity of exports or export/output ratio has been set; the conditions are merely that production be "export oriented". The value of the foreign partner's contribution should be not less than 1.5 million dinars (approximately US $ 100,000).

Management organs of joint venture operations include a joint venture manager and a joint operations board, whose functioning is specified in the contract. The joint venture manager and the director of the enterprise are the same person except when the foreign partner invests in a division of an existing enterprise; only in the latter case can the manager be a non-Yugoslav. The joint operations board is normally responsible for carrying out the terms of the contract within the limitation imposed by the retention of certain basic decisions with the workers' council. Powers that must remain with the workers' council, a self-management organ found in all enterprises, include legislative decisions (enterprise by-laws and statutes), personal and net income allocations, labor relations, and decisions concerning production, marketing and research activities[1].

The repatriation of the foreign partner's share of the profits, after taxation, is guaranteed by law subject to the constraint that the foreign exchange for profit repatriation be earned by the joint venture through exports. An incentive to export is thus provided, to the extent that the foreign investor wishes to repatriate his profits. Recent foreign exchange regulations permit Yugoslav enterprises to retain a minimum of 20 percent of their gross export earnings (cf. Chapter III). Joint venture operations are permitted to use an additional 33 percent of export earnings for the transfer of profits or invested capital. Transfers may take place only in the currencies of the accrued

---

[1] The management of the joint venture enterprise is thoroughly discussed in Sukijasović [1973b]. - A decree enacted in 1976 reiterates the requirement that foreign investment be export oriented, limits the equipment share of foreign investment to one-third of the value of the investment and the know-how share to 10 percent of the realized production during the duration of the joint venture agreement, and spells out specific matters which must remain outside the jurisdiction of the joint management board. The provisions of the decree are expected to be included in a new Law on Foreign Investment, which is due to be enacted in 1977.

export earnings. A part of the joint venture's annual depreciation allowance may also be used to repatriate invested capital.

In accordance with legislation enacted in 1971, the authority to tax the profits of foreign investors was shifted from the Federal to the Republic level. The tax rate is not uniform between the various Republics; the rate also varies with the share of reinvested profits. Current tax rates are presented in Table 39.

Table 39 - Tax Rates on Foreign Investors' Profits, 1975 (percent)

Republic	Percentage of profits reinvested			
	0	up to 25	25-50	50-100
Macedonia	14.0	11.2	8.4	5.6
Montenegro	14.0	11.9	9.8	7.0
Bosnia and Hercegovina	20.0	17.0	14.0	10.0
Croatia	35.0	29.75	24.5	17.5
Serbia	35.0	29.75	24.5	17.5
Slovenia	35.0	29.75	24.5	17.5

Source: Yugoslav Life [Vol. 22, 1975, No. 8-9, p. 5].

3. Growth and Structure of Foreign Investment

a. Growth of Foreign Investment

The removal of the barriers to foreign direct investment in 1967 did not result in a great gush of such investment. The lack of enthusiastic response from abroad is not surprising. One would expect potential investors from both the East and West to approach joint investment with Yugoslav enterprises with no small amount of caution. Western firms engaging in joint ventures with Yugoslav enterprises would be treading on new ground, which implies a relatively high degree of risk and uncertainty would be associated with the joint investment. The success of a joint venture between a capitalist firm and a worker-managed, socially owned domestic enterprise operating in a unique self-managed economy which had just undergone major reforms could not be obvious. The eastern Europeans also had cause for skepticism. Since 1948 they had looked upon the Yugoslavs and their unconventional economic system with much suspicion.

Table 40 - Foreign Investment in Yugoslavia[a], 1968-1973

Year	Number of contracts	Joint-venture investment			
		foreign share	Yugoslav share	total	foreign share
		million US $			percent
1968	3	12.5	41.7	54.2	23.1
1969	8	19.7	49.2	68.9	28.6
1970	12	17.2	64.3	81.5	21.1
1971	17	18.2	50.1	68.3	26.6
1972	26	37.9	286.9	324.8	11.7
1973	25	29.7	161.8	191.5	18.4
1968-1973	91	135.2	654.0	789.2	17.1

[a] Does not include 8 contracts which were registered but were terminated either without being realized at all or after an abbreviated period of time.

Source: Compiled from data in OECD [Foreign Investment 1974, pp. 38-56].

Following the registration of the first contract on April 3, 1968, a total of eleven contracts were registered during 1968-1969 (Table 40). Foreign investment during these first two years amounted to US $ 32.2 million, which was 26.2 percent of the joint venture investment (foreign plus Yugoslav partner contributions) during this period. Steps were soon taken to stimulate the investment of foreign capital in Yugoslavia. In late 1969 the International Investment Corporation for Yugoslavia (IICY) was formed. The IICY helps to find partners for domestic or foreign firms interested in joint venture investment in Yugoslavia. It also assists in the negotiations between prospective partners, and helps in the financial arrangements of the undertaking by providing its own funds or arranging other financing. The IICY's shareholders include the International Finance Corporation, 13 Yugoslav banks and 42 foreign banks from ten industrialized countries and Kuwait. As of mid-1973, 15 joint ventures had been sponsored by the IICY, with a total capital investment of US $ 343 million, of which the share of the foreign partner was US $ 56.6 million [OECD, Foreign Investment 1974, pp. 31 sq.].

Major liberalization of the foreign investment regulations took place during 1970-1971. The changes included 1) relaxation of the permanency conditions concerning foreign investment, 2) dropping the initial requirement that 20 percent of profits be reinvested in the Yugoslav economy, 3) an easing of the conditions regarding the repatriation of invested capital, and 4) protection of the foreign investor against the possibility of more stringent legislation being enacted following the formation of the joint venture[1]. The regulations pertaining to foreign investment in Yugoslav enterprises were consolidated in 1973 and incorporated in the Law on Foreign Investment in Domestic Organizations of Associated Labor[2]. A new Law on Foreign Investment is expected to be enacted in 1977 (footnote 1, p. 114).

The risk of investing in Yugoslavia has been reduced by arrangements made in the United States, as well as several other countries, to insure such investment. Agreements reached in January 1973 provide that United States private investment in Yugoslavia may be insured against non-commercial risks by the United States government's Overseas Private Investment Corporation (OPIC). In addition to providing insurance against non-commercial risks, OPIC provides investment counceling and makes and guarantees loans. Lack of insurance was said to have been a big hindrance to American investment in Yugoslavia; e.g., it was cited as the reason a joint operation involving a contribution of US $ 200 million by an American firm was not realized[3]. Steps to provide insurance for investment in Yugoslavia have been taken by France, the Federal Republic of Germany and others.

The value of foreign investment held fairly stable during 1969-1971, although the annual number of contracts registered with the Federal Secretariat of the Economy rose steadily from 8 in 1969 to 17 in 1971.

---

[1] Law on Foreign Investment in Domestic Organizations of Associated Labor [Official Gazette, No. 22/73]. - This provision has also been incorporated into the Yugoslav Constitution of 1974 [Article 27]: "The rights of foreign persons to resources invested in an organization of associated labor in the Socialist Federal Republic of Yugoslavia may not be restricted by statute or another enactment after the contract from which these rights stem has become legally valid."

[2] Changes in foreign investment regulations have occurred in the form of constitutional amendments, as well as by way of new or amended legislation, e.g., Amendments to the Law on Resource of Economic Organizations [Official Gazette, No. 34/71], Law on Foreign Exchange Operations [Official Gazette, No. 36/72], and Law on Foreign Investment in Domestic Organizations of Associated Labor [Official Gazette, No. 22/73]. See also the 1974 Constitution [Article 27].

[3] Sukijasović [1973b, p. 123]. - U.S. firms participated in 6 joint ventures in 1973 after having been involved in only 2 prior to 1973 (not including 3 joint ventures between foreign subsidiaries of U.S. firms and Yugoslav enterprises).

However, a spurt in foreign investment activity occurred in 1972, when the value of foreign investment of US $ 37.9 million was more than double the amount in 1971. There was a decline in 1973, but the sum still remained 50 percent greater than in any pre-1972 year. At least 31 contracts were concluded in 1974, the largest annual number of any year up to that time. Although the amount of foreign investment in Yugoslavia totaled only US $ 137.3 million as of January 31, 1974, an upward trend is evidenced[1]. This rising trend reflects both increasing investor confidence as more and more joint operations become operational, and function without major problems, and the evolvement of more favorable conditions (in both Yugoslavia and the home country of the foreign investor) for foreign investment in Yugoslavia. Total approved foreign investment during 1968-1973 amounted to .8 percent of total domestic economic investment in the social sector during the same period; foreign investment in the industrial sector came to 2.7 percent of domestic industrial investment during 1968-1973.

b. Structure of Foreign Investment

When viewed from the standpoint of the Yugoslav two-digit industrial classification, the metal products industry has attracted the most foreign investment (this will likely change in 1976; see footnote below). Almost one-half of foreign investment has been invested in this one industry (Table 41). Three quarters of foreign investment has gone to the metal products, chemical, rubber and electrical machinery and supplies industries (in descending order of magnitude). The electrical power, coal, shipbuilding, leather and footwear, and motion picture industries have attracted no foreign investment. When investment in the 15 industry branches of Table 41 is disaggregated into

---

[1] Following a year of negotiations, Dow Chemical Co. of the United States reached agreement with Industrija Nafte (INA) of Zagreb in March 1976, on a 49 percent participation in a US $ 750 million petro-chemical joint venture to be called Dina. This is the biggest American investment in eastern Europe. Data availability precludes the inclusion of joint ventures completed during the past two years in the analysis of this chapter. The amount of foreign investment in Yugoslavia is not particularly small when compared with two southern European countries, Turkey and Greece. It does appear low in comparison to the experiences of two other southern European countries, Spain and Portugal. Foreign investment in these countries, in millions of U.S. dollars, was as follows: Turkey (1959-1967) 70, Greece (1959-1967) 145, Spain (1960-1970) 1,168, and Portugal (1959-1970) 695 [UN, Economic Bulletin, Vol. 23, 1972, No. 2, p. 68].

Table 41 - Foreign Investment by Industry Branch, January 31, 1974

Industry	Number of contracts	Joint-venture investment				
		foreign share	Yugoslav share	total	foreign share	structure of foreign share
		US $			percent	
Crude petroleum	1	5,444,185	5,230,769	10,674,954	49.0	3.8
Ferrous metals	4	239,552,671	5,277,951	244,830,622	2.2	3.8
Non-ferrous metals	2	31,351,196	3,386,167	34,737,363	9.7	2.5
Non-metallic minerals	4	9,173,144	4,646,953	13,820,097	33.6	3.4
Metal products	31	194,302,721	63,372,607	257,675,328	24.6	46.2
Electrical machinery, etc.	11	50,378,603	8,284,362	58,662,965	14.1	6.0
Chemicals	17	46,726,578	21,447,705	68,174,283	31.5	15.6
Building materials	3	498,706	292,941	791,647	37.0	.2
Wood products	1	8,564,521	1,760,000	10,324,521	17.0	1.3
Paper and paper products	5	34,673,937	6,493,815	41,167,752	15.8	4.7
Textiles	4	1,225,040	1,190,003	2,415,043	49.3	.9
Rubber products	4	21,195,653	10,458,713	31,654,366	33.0	7.6
Food products	3	7,037,299	1,087,725	8,125,024	13.4	.8
Printing and publishing	1	127,500	122,500	250,000	49.0	.1
Tobacco manufactures	1	173,986	115,991	289,977	40.0	.1
Agriculture	1	158,010	151,813	309,823	49.0	.1
Construction and turn-key projects	1	6,545,723	2,812,615	2,358,338	30.1	2.0
Tourism	3	7,425,599	1,159,154	8,584,753	13.5	.8
Total	97	664,555,073	137,291,785	801,846,858	17.1	100

Source: See Table 40.

32 sectors, the motor vehicle industry, with about 39 percent of total foreign investment in industry, comes out as the leading sector; basic chemicals and rubber products follow in that order (Table A 18).

Turning to the structure of foreign investment by regions within Yugoslavia, about four-fifths of foreign capital has been invested in the republics of Slovenia and Serbia (Table 42). Only about 14 percent of the total has been invested in the less developed republics of Bosnia-Herzegovina, Montenegro and Macedonia, and the less developed autonomous province of Kosovo. The concentration of foreign investment in the richer republics exists despite the previously noted lower profits taxes found in the poorer regions. Foreign investment in Yugoslavia appears to be pulled toward those regions where the infrastructure is more highly developed, the level of industrialization is higher, the industrial labor force is larger and more experienced, and supplies of energy and raw materials are more favorable.

Table 42 - Regional Structure of Foreign Investment, January 1, 1973

Republic	Number of contracts	Percentage of total foreign investment
Bosnia-Herzegovina	6	7.0
Croatia	15	7.7
Macedonia	3	3.7
Serbia total	19	40.7
Serbia proper	14	38.5
Kosovo	2	.8
Vojvodina	3	1.4
Slovenia	27	38.7
Montenegro	1	2.2
Total	71	100

Source: Sukijasović [1973a, p. 53].

The major source of foreign investment has been western Europe (Table 43). This area has provided approximately 70 percent of the foreign capital invested in Yugoslavia. Not surprisingly, neighbor Italy and the Federal Republic of Germany, western Europe's leading industrial power, have been the leading investor countries, with 21.8 and 20.4 percent of the total, respectively[1]. The 30 percent of foreign investment that originated from non-western European countries was about equally divided between the United States, eastern Europe and international organizations. The country pattern of foreign investment reflects such factors as geographical location, labor market conditions, and institutional factors concerning the transfer of capital, e.g., freedom of capital exports, foreign investment insurance and the existence of multinational corporations.

[1] The recent Dow Chemical - INA agreement boosts the United States into the leading position in terms of amount invested.

Table 43 - Foreign Investment in Yugoslavia by Country, January 31, 1974

Countries	Joint-venture investment				
	foreign share	Yugoslav share	total	foreign share	structure of foreign share
	US $			percent	
Austria	7,606,863	70,461,824	78,068,687	9.7	5.5
Belgium	3,234,967	46,910,625	50,145,592	6.5	2.4
Czechoslovakia	3,630,769	4,627,692	8,258,469	44.0	2.6
Denmark	268,934	371,339	640,273	42.0	.2
France	13,324,309	37,615,292	50,939,601	26.4	9.7
Germany, Democratic Republic	8,510,769	8,880,000	17,390,769	48.9	6.2
Germany, Federal Republic	28,057,121	270,625,845	298,682,966	9.4	20.4
Great Britain	1,839,008	8,086,761	9,925,769	18.5	1.3
Italy	29,874,821	121,631,307	151,506,128	19.7	21.8
Netherlands	1,571,730	1,635,882	3,207,612	49.0	1.1
Sweden	3,670,385	11,424,444	15,094,829	24.3	2.7
Switzerland	6,840,591	13,080,879	19,921,470	34.3	5.0
United States	15,281,548	65,944,861	81,226,409	18.8	11.1
Other	13,579,970	3,258,318	16,838,288	80.6	9.9
Total	137,291,785	664,555,073	801,846,858	17.1	100

Source: See Table 40.

4. Motivations of the Foreign Investor

Foreign firms may decide to participate in joint ventures in Yugoslavia for two broad reasons: to produce for the Yugoslav market or for export. Turning first to a joint operation to serve the domestic market, producing in Yugoslavia avoids the problem of surmounting tariff and non-tariff barriers. The inducement to invest may also arise from cost advantages associated with labor costs or proximity to raw material supplies. The foreign firm may also engage in joint investment to get the jump on competitors or to protect or enlarge its share of the domestic market; the product cycle phenomenon may be relevant here as foreign investors strive to get a headstart in the production of goods which are in the standardization stage of their life cycle[1].

The cost factors cited above may also be associated with export-oriented foreign investment. Yugoslavia's location may also serve to attract foreign investment from United States firms interested in servicing the western and/or eastern European markets. Together with its location, Yugoslav experience in trading with eastern European nations is an asset to western firms interested in entering the market or expanding sales in eastern Europe[2]. The eastern European market accounts for about 40 percent of Yugoslavia's exports of manufactured goods. With the increasing negative reaction in western Europe to the inflow of foreign workers, firms in these countries can be expected to give greater consideration to the development of production facilities in the home countries of migrant workers. Additionally, Yugoslavia's non-aligned posture helps to make her an attractive place for exports to the developing countries, where some of the world's fastest industrial growth can be expected to take place.

To the extent that the foreign investor wishes to repatriate his share of the profits of the joint venture, all investment is at least partially export oriented[3]. Moreover, approval of proposed joint ventures does require evidence that a "significant" part of the joint operation's production will be exported. An analysis of the motivation of the foreign investor based on enterprise production and sales data is precluded by the small number of joint ventures which are operational and the dearth of data on those that are in operation. However, the question as to whether foreign investment is primarily domestic market or export oriented will be approached from another direction.

---

[1] For a survey of factors affecting the international location of production, see Dunning [1973]. - The product cycle model was developed by Vernon [1966]. - Foreign investment in industries at the mature stage of their product cycle may be export as well as domestic market oriented.

[2] For example, a director of the Dunlop Co. of the United Kingdom, which is involved in a joint venture with the Yugoslav enterprise FADIP, in explaining why Dunlop invested in the joint operation, said "There are many people here at Dunlop who feel that East-West trade will increase, and one must learn how to do the business." [Yugoslav Life, Vol. 20, 1975, No. 8-9, p. 6].

[3] Some foreign partner firms do not look upon exports with a great deal of favor. Possible reasons for this attitude are first, exports might replace production from other operations of the firm and second, sales in the domestic market may be more profitable. See, e.g., Ekonomska Politika [November 11, 1974].

Domestic market oriented foreign investment can be expected to be associated with such industry characteristics as the degree of protection, and the rate of growth of production. It is hypothesized that, ceteris paribus, domestic market oriented foreign investment will be positively associated with these variables. Considering only tariffs as protective devices, and viewing the tariff as a part of the cost of production of goods produced outside the country, the higher this cost becomes, the more difficult it is for imports to compete with domestically produced goods. Thus as foreign investment became possible in 1967, foreign firms which were not competitive in the Yugoslav market because of tariffs, might now consider obtaining a share of the market by investing in a joint venture.

Export-oriented foreign investment, on the other hand, is more under the influence of a different set of factors. Here decisions on where to locate production hinge on such conditions as labor costs, transport and distance costs, tariff barriers, government policies and risk[1]. As noted above, Yugoslavia is well situated for supplying the eastern and western European markets[2]. Assuming Yugoslavia to be a labor-abundant country, costs of production are posited to be relatively low for (especially unskilled) labor-intensive products[3].

In an attempt to provide information on the motive of the foreign investor as between producing for the domestic or foreign market, five industry characteristics were considered. The Spearman rank correlation coefficient was computed between foreign investment by industry branch (15 branches) and each of the following characteristics: capital/labor ratio, skill-intensity, export/output ratio, tariff rate and growth rate (Table 44). The first three characteristics are included to test for evidence of export orientation, the latter two for domestic market orientation.

---

[1] For more on this, see Helleiner [1973, pp. 35-40].

[2] A trade agreement with the EEC and inclusion in its generalized preference scheme together with associate member status with COMECON add to Yugoslavia's locational advantages for supplying the markets of these trade blocs.

[3] The assumption that labor is scarce relative to capital in Yugoslavia was discussed in Chapters I and IV. Low labor costs were found to be a major consideration concerning export-oriented foreign investment in Taiwan, while they had no significance in so far as domestic market oriented investment was concerned [Helleiner 1973, p. 44]. - See also Riedel [1975a, pp. 507 sqq.].

Table 44 - Spearman Rank Correlation Coefficients Between Foreign Investment in 15 Industries and Selected Industry Variables, 1967-1972

Capital/Labor[a]	Skill-intensity[b]	Export/Output[c]	Tariff[d]	Growth rate[e]
.1250	.4750*	.0714	.5250*	.5893*

[a] 1968. - [b] 1968. Personnel with secondary education and above, highly skilled and skilled per employee. - [c] Average 1970, 1972. - [d] 1971. - [e] 1967, 1972. - * Significant at least at the .05 level. Others are not significant at the .10 level.

Source: Capital/labor: SZzS [Medjubsobni odnosi privrednih delatnosti SFRJ 1968]. - SZzS [Statistički godišnjak SFRJ 1970, pp. 120 sq.]. - Skill-intensity: SZzS [Industrijska preduzeća 1970, Table 6]. - Export/output: SZzS [Statistički godišnjak SFRJ 1971, 1973, Table 106.5]. - SZzS [Statistika spoljne trgovine SFRJ 1972, Tables 1-10, 1-11]. - Tariff: World Bank [1975, p. 266]. - Growth rate: SZzS [Statistički godišnjak SFRJ 1974, Table 109.9].

The capital/labor ratio is used as a measure of the relative labor cost advantage of the various industries; lower capital/labor ratios are expected to be associated with larger amounts of export-oriented foreign investment. Rather than being negative as hypothesized, the Spearman coefficient is positive but not significantly different from zero. Assuming the export/output ratio to be reflective of the export prospects of an industry, export-oriented foreign investment should be greater in those industries with higher export/output ratios. The Spearman coefficient in this case is very close to zero. With respect to the skill-intensity variable, the assumption is that it is unskilled labor that is relatively abundant in Yugoslavia, with skilled labor being relatively scarce (cf. p. 126). This time the Spearman coefficient is significant (at the .05 level), but instead of being negative, as hypothesized, it is positive, implying that foreigners tend to invest more in skilled as opposed to unskilled labor-intensive industries. Thus the evidence does not support the proposition that foreign investment in Yugoslavia is mainly export oriented.

Turning now to investment for the domestic market, higher levels of investment are expected to be associated with higher tariff rates. Here the Spearman coefficient is positive and significant. It is also positive, as expected, and significant for the industry growth rate. The rationale for hypothesizing a positive correlation between foreign investment and the industry growth rate is that foreign firms which have the goal of maximizing their growth rates will be attracted toward the more rapidly expanding industries.

The evidence in Table 44 does not show foreign investment to be primarily export oriented. There is some indication that it is the possibility of extending or maintaining one's share of the domestic market, or getting a headstart on one's competitors in this market, that exerts the stronger pull on the investor[1]. This is consistent with a recent study in which it was stated that foreign investors have found the domestic market to be the most profitable, followed in order by the western and eastern European markets [Holt 1973, p. 62]. If in fact foreign investment has been export oriented, as the legal basis for such investment implies, the supporting evidence must be found elsewhere.

---

[1] Similar findings resulted when the value of foreign investment by industry branch was regressed on the capital/labor ratio and the tariff level. The resulting regression equation is as follows (with t values in parentheses):

$$FDI_i = -12,419 + 27,955\,R_i + 2,103\,T_i$$
$$(-1.317) \quad (.257) \quad (3.160)$$

$$R^2 = .372 \qquad D.W. = 2.943$$

where FDI is foreign investment in thousands of US \$, R is the capital/labor ratio in million dinars per man-year, T is the tariff rate and i is the industry branch. The simple correlation coefficients between the dependent variable and R_i and T_i are -.119 and .678, respectively. In addition, the value of foreign investment according to the 32 sectors in Table A 18 was regressed on the tariff rate, non-wage value-added per employee and wage value-added per employee. The latter two variables were used as proxies for capital-intensity and skill-intensity, respectively. Various combinations of the three independent variables were used in the estimations. However, in no case were the coefficients significant; the R^2 did not exceed .06. The simple correlation coefficients between foreign investment and the tariff rate, non-wage and wage value-added per employee were .227, -.003 and .084, respectively.

Foreign investment in Yugoslavia may be more export oriented than the preceding evidence implies. As previously stated, something like 40 percent of manufactured exports goes to eastern Europe. The percentage is even higher for exports of those industries in which foreign investment is concentrated, namely, the automotive, chemical and electrical machinery industries. For example, in 1972, 47 percent of machinery and transport equipment exports, other than ships, went to eastern Europe, as well as 61 percent of exports of chemicals. Much of this trade is governed by trade agreements and is not subject to the price and quality competition that exists in trade with other regions. The Yugoslav exporter frequently accepts "compensation in kind", "switch deals", or "reciprocal deliveries"[1]. In other cases, the foreign partner is compelled to purchase part of the joint venture's production and dispose of it in a hard currency country or use it elsewhere within its own organization in order to be able to transfer its profits.

As noted in Chapter V, Yugoslavia's comparative advantage vis-à-vis eastern Europe and the less developed countries is less likely to be in traditional labor-intensive industries in which Yugoslavia could be expected to have a comparative cost advantage in trade with western industrialized countries. Another point to consider is the relatively compressed wage structure found in Yugoslav enterprises. As previously pointed out, the average personal income of the highest paid university educated workers in 1966 was 2.73 times greater than the average income of the lowest paid unskilled workers (footnote 1, p. 10). An implication of this narrow wage structure is that skilled workers are relatively underpaid when compared to unskilled workers. The country may thus be more internationally competitive in skilled labor-intensive goods than would be judged from a consideration of the relative physical abundance of skilled labor in Yugoslavia[2].

---

[1] The difference between compensation in kind and reciprocal deliveries is that the former involves goods for which the receiver has no use and thus must find a market for, while the latter consists of goods which can be used in the firm's production or distribution network. Switch deals involve accepting a third party obligation. See Holt [1973, pp. 55 sq.] for more on these types of export deals.

[2] See also the reference in footnote 2, p. 10, to the relative cheapness of skilled and unskilled labor in Iran and Yugoslavia. In addition, see the discussion in Chapter I of the capital-intensive bias of worker management and implications for comparative advantage.

Also worthy of consideration is Yugoslavia's economic and social position somewhere between East and West. This provides certain advantages concerning production for the eastern European market which can dominante factor-price considerations. An official of a western firm recently wrote: "Yugoslavia does send the largest percentage of its exports to the socialist countries so firms here are attractive as joint venture partners. Overall, Yugoslavia is a socialist country but it is much freer than other socialist countries. And, its methods of doing business are much more Western and open. Many Western and Japanese businessmen look on Yugoslavia as a half-way country, i.e., a country to demonstrate their products for other socialist nations" [Hartz 1974, p. 36]. This same official, who negotiated a joint venture with a Yugoslav enterprise, noted that part of his firm's profits from the joint venture would be received in the form of the production of the joint operation. A representative of another American firm comments that the only way he can sell in volume in eastern Europe is to do the manufacturing there. Because of market size and technical requirements, Yugoslavia is the preferred location [Hartz 1974, p. 36].

Limited information on joint ventures which have become operational indicates production has been both domestic market and export oriented[1]. Two joint operations in the automotive industry are not emphasizing exports because of strong domestic demand. The foreign partner of another joint operation is under obligation to market 40 percent of production abroad. One joint venture in the electrical industry is exporting 90 percent of its output. Projected exports of 60 percent of the output of a chemical joint operation were not realized because of the strength of domestic demand. Four other chemical enterprises have set export targets ranging between 20 and 90 percent of production. Information on one or two joint ventures in each of the paper, textile, rubber and tobacco industries indicates actual or projected exports of 35-60 percent of output. Here again the strength of domestic demand prevented export targets being reached in some instances.

In spite of the export-oriented nature of Yugoslav foreign investment legislation, the orientation of foreign investment toward producing for the domestic market appears at least as strong as producing for exports. Data on actual export performance is unfortunately extremely sparse. More specific information on a larger number of firms for

[1] This information on joint venture performance is taken from Sukijasović [1973b, pp. 235-237].

a longer time period is necessary before firm conclusions concerning the motivation of the foreign investor can be reached. It should also be noted that the industries that have attracted the most foreign investment are also among the more import-intensive in production[1]. Thus careful calculation is required to determine the net balance-of-trade effect of joint-venture exports.

[1] In the twenty-industry industrial sector, the rubber, chemical, electrical machinery and metal products industries ranked 2, 4, 7 and 10, respectively, in terms of import (direct plus indirect) intensity of production in 1970 [see Sekulić 1972, p. 140]. Import intensity refers to the share of direct and indirect imported inputs in the value of production (this concept is discussed in Chapter V).

Chapter VII: Conclusions and a Look Beyond

Yugoslavia has made significant economic progress under her unique self-management system. A journey through the country's major urban centers conveys the impression that a new member of the club of so-called developed nations is emerging. Stores are attractively filled with consumer goods, many of which are imported or produced in Yugoslavia under some type of cooperation with foreign firms. Most makes and types of automobiles can be seen on the streets, from the locally produced Fiat 750 joint-venture product to the snobbish Mercedes. The numerous travel agencies are crowded with anxious travellers. Regardless of what per capita income comparisons might imply, the visible standard of living is high in Yugoslavia in relation to other eastern European countries[1]. The Yugoslavs are obviously enjoying the fruits of their labor.

The old proverb "He who hesitates is lost", may be an apt description of the Yugoslav consumer. An explanation of this behavior could be the recent high rate of inflation which makes putting money into savings accounts unattractive, and the lack of alternative savings possibilities. Given the negative real rate of return on savings accounts, the absence of a securities market and the lack of property investment opportunities (except in one's apartment or house), it is not surprising to see a rush to consumption. Spending on consumer durables is especially attractive in such circumstances.

It is not meant to be implied that Yugoslavia has solved all of her problems; far from it in fact. Severe poverty and backwardness can be found in areas of the country. The system of worker rewards leaves something to be desired in the way of motivation and efficiency. Housing standards are not high. Other causes of concern are the level of unemployment, price instability and balance-of-payments disequilibrium.

The economic gains made to date, however, take on added significance when it is realized that the trail of progress began from a position of destruction. In addition, the history of the country is not one of a united people who customarily pulled together - not even during World War II. Thus the picture of a country of workers and peasants with a divided history pulling themselves up largely by their own bootstraps to a position of respectability is a significant achievement.

---

[1] The same relationship may not exist insofar as social services, including housing, are concerned.

The accomplishments, however, have not been achieved in the absence of outside help. For example, United States aid of $ 2 billion was provided during 1949-1961[1]. Most of this aid was in the form of grants; it helped to make possible the low ratio of exports to imports that existed during this period (see Table 22). More recently the source of capital inflow has been less concentrated and its form has shifted toward loans rather than grants. As noted in Chapter V, net medium and long-term capital inflow averaged US $ 200 million during 1961-1972. The non-aligned political posture of the country puts it in a position to draw on both the East and West for capital inflows; in practice, however, Yugoslavia's eastern European neighbors have made only meager foreign aid contributions. It should also be kept in mind that the economic blockade imposed by the eastern European countries in effect was a form of negative economic assistance. Additionally, economic growth has taken place in an environment of frequent and major institutional change and experimentation, making uninterrupted progress more difficult.

This study has shown not only that rapid economic growth and institutional change can go hand-in-hand, but also that policies of import substitution and export expansion are not necessarily mutually exclusive. It was revealed that import substitution policies were partially thwarted by a high import intensity of production in import substitution industries. Import substitution industries are also found among the major export sectors. An explanation of this tendency is the existence of excess capacity in those industries; exports (subsidized) were thus a way of increasing capital utilization. It was also suggested that policies toward primary industries contributed to input shortages and an inflated import intensity in industries at higher levels of processing. Some of the major export sectors were also shown to be highly import intensive in production. Despite the existence of import substitution policies, industrialization has taken place under conditions of a reasonable degree of outward orientation of the economy. The growth of total (manufactured) exports has been more rapid than that of aggregate (industrial) production. Manufactured exports have been particularly dynamic. Nevertheless, more progress is desired in this area. Export promotion policy has been less than satisfactory in terms of taking full account of the nation's comparative advantage. This is invariably a difficult policy area for industrializing countries. Com-

---

[1] World Bank [1975, p. 289]. - Of the US $ 2 billion total, about $ 700 million consisted of military assistance. The aid amounted to 28 percent of the value of imports during 1949-1961.

plicating factors include the issue of static versus dynamic comparative advantage and the weight to attach to demand considerations. Investment policy can also be criticized as having been overly subject to political considerations.

In looking to the future, fundamental institutional changes again appear to be taking place. Much of the blame for the growing structural imbalance (associated with increasing import dependence), economic instability and general decline in economic performance that has taken place since the enonomic reforms of the mid-1960's has officially been ascribed to the system of indicative planning and to an over-reliance on a freely functioning market[1]. New laws designed to remedy the defects in the economic system and to bring the system into conformity with the Constitution of 1974 are currently being debated and enacted. Only an outline of the changes in the planning and foreign trade systems will be presented here. More detailed analysis must await completion of the legislative process and the implementation of the laws.

Under the new system of planning, called self-management planning, which was codified in a new law on planning in 1976, all economic units are involved in the planning process. The planning process begins with the passage of a law on planning, which includes a list of minimum indicators. Planning begins simultaneously at all levels. Each enterprise or basic organization of associated labor (BOAL) projects its sales and purchases over the planning period, e.g., five years, and shares this information with other enterprises[2]. Through an iterative process, the plans of all these economic units are harmonized. The harmonization culminates in binding self-management agreements which link together enterprises that are related vertically (through forward or backward linkages) or horizontally in the production process[3]. Economic chambers play a role in the harmonization proce-

---

[1] Whether in fact the major cause of the difficulties was a failure of the market mechanism or inadequate economic policy (e.g., providing the market with faulty signals) is subject to debate.

[2] The Five-Year Plan is assessed and adjusted annually.

[3] Self-management agreements may be concluded for a specific time period or without a specified time period. They may cover a range of matters, e.g., distribution of jointly earned income (between enterprises or within an enterprise), the formation of BOALs or enterprises, resource pooling, and the terms of inter- or intra-enterprise deliveries.

dure. A similar process takes place at the level of socio-political communities resulting in the conclusion of social compacts[1]. A continuous integrating process takes place between the self-management and social plans[2]. Thus the new planning system calls for wide participation in the planning process.

A new Law on Foreign Exchange Resources is currently working its way through the legislative process after a long period of discussion. This Law is expected to contain two significant institutional changes: a system of linking imports to exports and a new method of distibuting foreign exchange earnings. The policy of linking imports to exports was adopted briefly in 1967. Its reintroduction in 1975 came as a reaction to a seriously deteriorating balance of payments situation. The balance of trade deficit of $ 3.7 billion in 1974 was more than twice its level in 1973. The deficit on current account in 1974 reached $ 1.2 billion, following surpluses in the previous two years[3]. This worsening balance of payments resulted from several simultaneously occurring factors: recession in the West, a sharp decline in the terms of trade (associated primarily with the rise in oil prices), the EEC ban on beef imports, and rapidly rising income and investment associated with a domestic economic boom.

The export-import linking has been applied to trade with convertible currency countries. It is the trade with these countries that accounts for the major share of Yugoslavia's balance of trade deficit. For example, trade with the OECD countries accounted for 75 percent of Yugoslavia's balance of trade deficit in 1974 and 89 percent in 1975. The share of the value of imports that must be covered by exports varies according to commodity; for imports of capital goods the share is 30 percent and for consumer goods the share is 100 percent. In some instances the foreign firm uses the compulsory imports in its production network; in other cases the foreign firm markets the goods or arranges for a Yugoslav export-import enterprise to do the marketing.

---

[1] Social compacts may deal with such issues as sector priorities and price, employment, foreign trade and income distribution policies.

[2] The planning process can be viewed as simultaneously planning from the top down and the bottom up, with convergence through harmonization. The planning from each direction is subject to certain constraints or goals, e.g., overall growth targets and outputs of certain priority sectors.

[3] The trade and current account deficits in 1975 were $ 3.6 billion and $ 1.0 billion, respectively.

Since the policy of export-import linking was implemented, the aggregate export/import ratio (in percent) increased from 50.6 in 1974 to 52.9 in 1975; indications are that the ratio will exceed 65 percent in 1976. Several factors contributed to this increase, including more rapid growth in the West, import restrictions and restrictive domestic economic policies. However, export-import linking must have made an important contribution. Some portion of the implied increase in costs to the foreign supplier associated with the linking is likely to be passed on to the Yugoslav importer. On the other hand, the wider exposure of Yugoslav products may increase exports through a demonstration effect.

Insofar as the distribution of foreign exchange earnings is concerned, the crucial provision of the new law is that foreign exchange earnings belong not only to the final exporter but must be shared by all enterprises (or BOALs) that contributed to the production of the good before it reached the final exporter. The foreign exchange shares of the direct and indirect exporters are to be identified in self-management agreements[1]. The foreign exchange retention quota will be discontinued when this new system of distributing foreign exchange is implemented. Significant also is a new policy providing for risk sharing by enterprises including export-import enterprises. An implication of this policy is that export-import enterprises will no longer be able to perform a purely marketing function but must share in risk and income.

Growth targets for the next Five-Year Plan (1976-1980) in annual percentages are:

Social product	7	Investment in fixed assets	8
Industry (social sector)	8	Exports (goods and services)	8
Agriculture (social sector)	4	Imports (goods and services)	4.5
Employment	3.5		

Energy (electricity, coal, petroleum and gas), agro-industry, metallurgy, non-metallic minerals, basic chemicals, shipbuilding, equipment, infrastructure and tourism have been singled out as priority sectors. The means for attainment of the goals of these sectors are specified in social compacts, which assure the necessary flow of resources to these industries. Investment and foreign trade policies are geared to meet the requirements of the priority sectors.

The list of priority industries suggests that special efforts will be made to alleviate the structural imbalance in the economy that has resulted in bottlenecks and a rising import dependence. The implied

[1] This principle of distributing foreign exchange is related to the concept of net total exports or exports out of value-added discussed in Chapter V.

Plan import elasticity of .6 is less than one-half its historical level. Import substitution is expected to be especially important in the growth of the basic chemicals, ferrous metals, equipment, and synthetic rubber industries. Whether both the aggregate growth and import targets can be achieved is highly problematical.

The export growth target appears to be more easily attainable than that of imports. Although projected export expansion is somewhat greater than what has been experienced during the past decade, it is not inconsistant with the longer-run trend. The growth of exports of course is highly dependent on world economic expansion and commercial policies.

Turning to somewhat longer-run development prospects, the main economic growth targets for 1976-1985 are as follows (in terms of annual percentage increase).

Social product	7	Exports (goods and services)	9
Industry	9	Imports (goods and services)	7
Agriculture	3	Employment	3.5

The development of the raw materials sector of the economy continues as a priority item in the long run. Other areas of long-run emphasis include stable growth of the social product, employment generation, infrastructure development and reduction of regional inequalities (1975 social product per capita in Slovenia of $ 2,826 was more than six times the $ 434 of the autonomous province of Kosovo)[1].

The export growth of 9 percent per annum seems not to be unreasonable. Total merchandise exports grew at an annual rate of 8.4 and manufactured exports at 10.3 percent during 1956-1975, when the social product was growing at a 7.2 percent rate and industrial production at 9.4 percent (in 1972 prices). Export expansion slackened during the past decade (1965-1975), as the growth rate of merchandise exports and manufactured exports was 5.4 and 6.2 percent, respectively. Should a growth rate of industrial production of 9 percent be achieved, industrial exports could conceivably expand at an annual rate approaching 9 percent[2]. This assumes, however, that the growth of world trade will not be too dissimilar from the trend of the past decade.

---

[1] For further information on long-run development plans, see Assembly of the Socialist Federal Republic of Yugoslavia, "Draft Outline of a Common Policy for Long-Term Development in Yugoslavia (until 1985)" [Yugoslav Survey, Vol. 16, 1975, No. 4, pp. 19-90].

[2] Support for the view that manufactured exports could well expand at an annual rate in double figures can also be found in Chapter V.

Optimism concerning the prospects for manufactured export expansion is associated with the fact that the "joint-venture effect" has hardly been felt up to now. One of the conditions for approval of a joint-venture contract is that the project should result in increased productivity and exports. Moreover, the transfer of profits is tied to export proceeds (cf. Chapter VI). However, during the first two-and-a-half years following the adoption of foreign investment legislation in July 1967, only 15 joint-venture contracts were registered. By the end of January 1974, the total investment in 97 joint-venture contracts came to $ 802 million, with 17 percent of this total representing foreign capital. In a recent development the American firm Dow Chemical Corporation and a Yugoslav firm reached agreement to build and operate a $ 750 million petro-chemical complex in Yugoslavia. Some of the output of this joint operation is expected to be exported, while a greater portion will substitute for imports. As more and more of the joint-venture projects become operational, a shot in the arm for manufactured export growth can be expected.

Future growth of foreign investment will depend to some extent on the success of other eastern European countries in attracting foreign capital. It will also depend on Yugoslav commercial policies. An increase in protectionism would provide greater impetus to domestic market-oriented foreign investment. A greater emphasis on import substitution could perhaps lead to the profit repatriation conditions being modified to encourage foreign exchange savings by the joint operation as well as foreign exchange earnings. Such a move would stimulate foreign investment but at some cost if part of an overall policy of greater protectionism.

This optimism concerning export prospects must be tempered by policies expected to be associated with the 1976-1980 Five-Year Plan. As pointed out above, while export promotion will continue, import substitution is going to be emphasized. This strengthening of the policy of import substitution has obvious implications for resource allocation and export competitiveness. Another cause of concern relates to the geographical orientation of foreign trade. Eastern Europe and the developing countries may provide the fastest growing markets for Yugoslav exports in the future. But given that a large part of trade with these areas is not settled in convertible currencies, a serious balance-of-payments problem could develop to the extent these clearing area exports contain a large import requirement from the convertible area.

The recent increase in oil prices also adds an element of complication. The value of oil imports rose to about $ 800 million in 1974, after being slightly less than $ 300 million in 1973 and about $ 100 million in 1972. The share of oil imports in total merchandise imports went from 4 percent in 1972 to 11 percent in 1974; about one-fifth of the balance-of-trade deficit in 1974 can be directly attributed to the oil import surplus. Nevertheless, Yugoslavia is not as dependent on oil imports for its fuel needs as many other countries. In contrast to western Europe's dependence on oil for over 60 percent of its primary energy consumption, Yugoslavia's oil dependence is less than 50 percent. Wood, coal and hydro-electric power are the major power sources for industrial energy requirements. Industrial branches with the highest direct and indirect petroleum requirements per unit of output are non-metallic minerals, rubber products, ferrous metallurgy, chemicals and building materials. With the exception of chemicals, none of these branches are major export industries. Thus structural domestic production changes in response to oil-price induced relative changes in costs and prices should not cause major shocks in the structure of manufactured exports.

The effects of a reverse in the net flow of emigrant workers are uncertain at this point. Not only is it not known how long the net return of these workers from western Europe, which is currently taking place, will continue, there also is an element of uncertainty concerning the likelihood of the outflow moving in another direction, i.e., toward eastern Europe and the developing countries (a flow which is currently taking place to some extent). The effects of returning workers on efficiency are also unclear. On the one hand, these workers will bring back acquired skills. But, on the other hand, existing enterprises face pressures to employ these workers and thus acquire (or add to the current numbers of) redundant workers.

The new Federal Constitution adopted in 1974 is ushering in a new phase in the economic planning system. Emphasis is to be on more planning, within and among enterprises, sectors, regions and Republics. Coordination is to be stressed - both horizontally, i.e., within industries, and vertically, i.e., between the various supplying and consuming activities. It is expected that a strengthening of the planning process will result, in contrast to recent experience where economic plans have had more formal than practical significance. How the new system will work, with the complexities involved in working up from the plans of the basic economic units to the national level, is not certain. The aims of the new system to bring about greater coordination and rationality in the economy are good. To what extent the goals will be realized is not obvious.

One thing seems fairly safe to predict. Experimentation and change will continue to be major features of the Yugoslav system as it attempts to solve its problems and break new growth paths. And while, as some Yugoslav economists are prone to say, nobody really knows how the system functions, it will likely continue to do so and also maintain its role of innovator.

Statistical Appendix

Table A 1 - Shares of Major Exports in Total Exports, 1921-1939 (annual averages in percentage of value of total exports)

Commodity	Time period			
	1921-1925	1926-1930	1931-1935	1936-1939
Weat and flour	8.8	9.7	4.4	7.7
Corn	10.2	7.1	8.6	6.4
Fresh and dried prunes	3.5	2.4	3.1	2.2
Tobacco	.2	.9	3.6	2.3
Hemp	1.6	1.3	1.8	3.8
Livestock	15.3	12.7	11.3	12.0
Meat	6.2	3.9	4.8	5.7
Eggs	6.8	7.2	5.1	2.7
Hides	2.3	1.8	1.8	2.5
Timber	17.3	20.0	18.8	15.5
Blister copper	2.8	5.0	7.9	8.0
Lead	1.3	1.0	1.0	-
Ores	1.0	1.5	2.5	2.1
Lead and zinc concentrates	-	-	-	3.5
Cement	1.9	2.0	2.1	1.0
Other	20.8	23.5	23.2	24.6
Total	100	100	100	100
Annual average total exports (million dinars)	6,529	7,073	3,828	5,304

Source: Adapted from Tomasevich [1949, p. 173].

Table A 2 - Shares of Major Imports in Total Imports, 1921-1939 (annual averages in percentage of value of total imports)

Commodity	Time period			
	1921-1925	1926-1930	1931-1935	1936-1939
Raw cotton	1.5	2.3	4.5	5.6
Cotton yarn and products	25.3	18.4	16.2	11.9
Other vegetable-fibre products	2.2	2.3	2.0	2.0
Raw wood	1.0	1.3	1.6	2.5
Woollen yarn and products	8.9	7.5	6.9	6.6
Silk and silk products	1.3	2.7	4.1	2.7
Hides and leather	3.9	3.9	3.2	2.3
Coffee	2.6	2.7	2.1	1.3
Rice	1.4	1.6	1.5	1.3
Petroleum products	3.4	3.0	2.3	2.2
Coal, anthracite, coke	2.6	2.6	2.6	2.8
Iron, steel and products	9.7	10.7	10.6	11.4
Machinery and tools	3.4	6.1	5.0	7.9
Electrotechnical products	1.2	2.2	3.3	3.5
Other	31.6	32.7	34.7	36.0
Total	100	100	100	100
Annual average total imports (million dinars)	7,170	7,461	3,563	4,761

Source: Adapted from Tomasevich [1949, p. 178].

Table A 3 - Index of Export and Import Volume, 1925-1939 (1956 = 100)

Year	Exports	Imports	Year	Exports	Imports
1925	109	66	1933	89	37
1926	117	64	1934	103	45
1927	102	65	1935	93	45
1928	101	82	1936	83	53
1929	117	80	1937	125	62
1930	115	78	1938	96	60
1931	88	62	1939	93	58
1932	69	39			

Source: Pertot [1970, pp. 10 sq.]

Table A 4 - Selected Indicators of Price Movements, 1952-1973

Year	Prices of manufactured goods[a]	Prices of agricultural goods[a]	Retail prices	Cost of living	Ratio of (1) : (2)	Rate of inflation[b]
	1966 = 100					percent
	(1)	(2)	(3)	(4)	(5)	(6)
1952	68	20	40	29	3.4	
1953	66	24	40	30	2.8	- .3
1954	65	25	38	29	2.6	13.0
1955	68	28	41	33	2.4	3.8
1956	69	29	43	36	2.4	10.5
1957	69	32	43	37	2.2	- .3
1958	69	33	44	38	2.1	-1.6
1959	70	32	45	39	2.2	4.5
1960	71	34	48	43	2.1	11.3
1961	74	39	52	46	1.9	10.4
1962	74	44	55	51	1.7	7.6
1963	75	48	58	54	1.6	8.0
1964	78	60	63	60	1.3	19.5
1965	90	86	81	81	1.0	28.4
1966	100	100	100	100	1.0	14.7
1967	102	97	107	107	1.1	2.1
1968	103	93	112	112	1.1	3.8
1969	106	102	120	121	1.0	6.7
1970	116	117	131	134	1.0	12.4
1971	133	143	151	155	.9	19.4
1972	148	183	174	181	.8	14.7
1973	167	229	207	217	.7	18.5

[a] Producers' prices. - [b] According to the implicit social product deflator.

Source: SZzS [Statistički godišnjak SFRJ 1971, 1974, Section 121]. - SZzS [Jugoslavija 1945-1964, Section 13].

Table A 5 - Average Tariffs by Branch of Production, 1967-1971

Industry	1967	1969	1971
Electrical energy	-	-	-
Coal and coke	.5	1.0	1.3
Petroleum	5.0	6.9	6.8
Ferrous metals	6.7	9.8	8.3
Non-ferrous metals	2.3	3.0	2.7
Non-metallic minerals	9.7	10.3	10.3
Metal products	24.0	25.1	21.3
Shipbuilding	1.8	1.1	1.7
Electrical equipment	20.4	21.7	19.4
Chemicals	7.9	10.1	9.8
Construction materials	3.1	5.2	4.2
Wood products	6.1	7.9	6.5
Pulp and paper	7.8	11.4	11.7
Textiles and clothing	9.1	11.2	11.6
Leather and footwear	10.8	13.1	13.4
Rubber products	9.1	7.6	10.5
Food processing	4.6	4.8	3.8
Printing	7.3	12.3	5.5
Tobacco manufactures	16.6	11.8	10.8
Motion pictures	2.3	6.2	3.3
Total industry	13.6	15.0	13.1
Agriculture	2.4	1.9	1.5
Forestry	.2	.7	.5
Grand total	12.3	13.9	12.1

Source: SZzS [O radu carinske službe za 1971 Godište].

Table A 6 - Nominal and Effective Tariffs, 1970 (percent)

Sector	Nominal tariff	Effective tariff
Energy	5.0	10.8
Ferrous and non-ferrous metals	4.9	11.2
Non-metallic minerals and products	8.0	11.6
Metal and electrical products	23.7	41.4
Chemicals and paper	11.7	27.8
Wood products	7.2	12.8
Leather and rubber	15.0	27.8
Food products	9.5	22.6
Miscellaneous industry	7.2	12.1
Agriculture	3.3	4.3
Forestry	1.0	.7

Source: Ekonomski Institut Ljubljana [1971].

Table A 7 - Annual Growth Rates of Social Product, Industrial Production and Agricultural Production, 1953-1973 (percent)

Year	Social product[a]	Industrial production	Agricultural production[b]
1953	20.0	11.0	42.6
1954	1.3	13.5	-10.4
1955	14.8	16.7	24.6
1956	-6.0	10.2	-17.4
1957	23.9	16.7	45.1
1958	1.6	11.1	-12.6
1959	21.6	13.3	32.2
1960	5.8	15.1	-10.1
1961	5.7	6.6	- 2.8
1962	4.2	7.5	2.9
1963	12.4	15.6	10.3
1964	11.5	16.0	5.9
1965	1.6	8.1	- 8.8
1966	8.5	4.2	15.8
1967	2.6	- .2	- .8
1968	4.0	6.3	- 3.8
1969	10.4	11.3	9.5
1970	6.1	9.1	- 4.3
1971	8.8	10.3	6.8
1972	4.6	7.9	- 2.1
1973	5.3	5.9	7.2

[a]In 1966 prices. - [b]Based on the index of agricultural production, 1954-1963 = 100.

Source: Calculated from data in: SZzS [Statistički godišnjak SFRJ 1971, Tables 105.1, 109.10; 1974, Tables 105.4, 107.4, 109.10]. - SZzS [Jugoslavija 1945-1964, Table 6.3].

Table A 8 - Index of Industrial Production, 1939-1973 (1952 = 100)

Industry	1939	1946	1947	1948	1949	1950	1951	1953	1954	1955	1956	1957	1958	1959
Electrical energy	43	43	54	76	82	89	95	111	127	161	184	231	272	300
Coal and coke	70	58	80	90	103	107	100	97	113	131	146	152	157	174
Crude petroleum	24	14	21	36	57	89	98	130	153	172	191	247	278	329
Ferrous metals	57	44	70	83	86	86	91	118	150	197	222	277	304	346
Non-ferrous metals	69	46	62	71	82	90	94	102	107	130	145	162	174	184
Non-metallic minerals	38	39	57	72	92	90	97	134	149	179	209	241	272	303
Metal products	38	35	58	76	92	101	100	127	139	161	170	199	224	267
Electrical machinery, etc.	12	18	28	52	73	72	78	132	155	198	229	310	378	464
Chemicals	61	42	73	88	97	98	100	108	134	179	217	256	314	400
Building materials	61	49	79	92	99	102	89	109	116	126	129	152	165	186
Wood products	81	55	86	117	138	144	118	106	110	119	121	140	150	180
Paper and paper products	72	66	84	95	101	103	106	114	122	149	207	233	248	275
Textiles	84	67	103	130	133	127	110	97	120	138	145	167	181	196
Leather and footwear	78	63	103	140	162	150	127	92	105	123	137	157	172	199
Rubber products	60	37	83	93	116	111	110	100	118	125	147	184	195	220
Food products	88	75	115	139	125	116	137	133	145	154	173	226	234	272
Tobacco manufactures	79	50	88	126	126	117	85	87	1[illegible]5	130	150	128	183	143
Total industry[a]	61	48	73	91	102	105	101	111	126	147	162	189	210	238

continued

Table A 8 continued

Industry	1960	1961	1962	1963	1964	1965	1966	1967	1968	1969	1970	1971	1972	1973
Electrical energy	330	367	417	500	524	573	633	689	761	853	968	1, 090	1, 217	1, 277
Coal and coke	184	191	190	209	223	224	219	197	200	197	204	223	224	227
Crude petroleum	439	561	662	724	828	981	1, 167	1, 277	1, 315	1, 469	1, 704	1, 951	1, 979	2, 107
Ferrous metals	388	405	416	430	473	508	533	528	576	637	725	810	877	938
Non-ferrous metals	207	228	261	285	294	312	321	333	356	393	416	426	472	528
Non-metallic minerals	356	389	432	388	594	647	695	686	741	860	955	1, 134	1, 082	1, 133
Metal products	327	342	342	387	486	526	523	501	525	603	669	722	745	805
Electrical machinery etc.	576	645	725	913	1, 205	1, 262	1, 320	1, 360	1, 484	1, 789	1, 916	2, 179	2, 383	2, 543
Chemicals	452	506	563	718	865	1, 049	1, 200	1, 218	1, 414	1, 727	2, 006	2, 336	2, 631	2, 870
Building materials	212	228	212	242	277	287	288	302	334	371	403	448	488	514
Wood products	208	228	254	287	339	363	373	357	377	413	441	492	532	541
Paper and paper products	328	404	491	583	720	830	894	982	1, 066	1, 140	1, 212	1, 319	1, 445	1, 541
Textiles	224	230	256	295	334	357	385	373	387	408	426	458	505	535
Leather and footwear	240	258	272	318	388	409	414	401	400	439	431	475	526	538
Rubber products	277	296	306	377	467	514	553	570	568	681	731	814	906	973
Food products	320	346	368	425	472	506	549	560	559	608	674	753	806	852
Tobacco manufactures	141	114	97	147	207	222	200	201	203	184	187	196	205	233
Total industry[a]	274	292	314	363	421	455	474	473	503	560	611	674	727	770

[a]Excluding military manufactures. Printing and publishing included from 1954 and shipbuilding from 1957.

Source: SZzS [Industrija 1973, p. 9].

Table A 9 - Sources of Industrial Growth[a], 1952-1970 (percent)

	1952-1956			1956-1961			1961-1965		
	IS	EE	DD	IS	EE	DD	IS	EE	DD
Electrical energy	21.6	11.3	67.1	7.2	3.6	89.2	- 9.1	29.2	79.9
Coal and coke	14.1	10.4	75.5	.04	10.4	89.6	29.6	9.2	61.2
Crude petroleum	39.1	3.5	57.4	24.4	7.9	67.7	- 3.4	17.2	86.2
Ferrous metals	74.4	25.2	.4	-57.6	18.0	139.6	34.7	23.9	41.4
Non-ferrous metals	34.1	-15.3	81.2	-66.5	29.0	137.5	26.2	51.8	22.0
Non-metallic minerals	33.9	19.5	46.6	-66.3	34.0	132.3	20.2	31.4	48.4
Metal products	55.0	6.2	38.8	-17.9	14.5	103.4	41.6	18.6	39.8
Shipbuilding	-19.0	31.2	87.8	7.6	22.4	70.0	- 8.7	95.0	13.7
Electrical machinery, etc.	65.8	6.2	28.0	- 1.4	16.1	85.3	30.2	20.3	49.5
Chemicals	21.4	9.2	69.4	8.9	9.3	81.8	30.9	18.9	50.2
Building materials	14.4	8.2	77.4	4.5	1.2	94.3	3.7	4.8	91.5
Wood products	6.9	25.6	67.5	- 4.7	21.6	83.1	4.4	25.8	69.8
Paper and paper products	38.9	9.8	51.3	-23.6	16.2	107.4	20.9	29.3	49.8
Textiles	4.2	33.8	62.0	-20.5	18.0	102.5	27.4	16.1	56.5
Leather and footwear	20.2	19.0	51.8	- .5	19.6	80.9	- 2.1	45.8	56.3
Rubber	38.2	0	61.8	15.8	3.2	81.0	17.9	10.9	71.2
Food products	28.3	.8	70.9	7.0	12.4	80.6	9.5	6.7	83.8
Printing, publishing	16.4	0	83.6	3.3	1.6	95.1	.4	3.6	96.0
Tobacco manufactures	0	38.2	61.8	0	-14.8	114.3	0	59.9	40.1
Motion pictures	-55.6	0	155.6	34.5	8.4	57.1	0	-910.0	1,010.0
Total[b]	26.9	17.4	55.8	-15.1	14.7	100.4	19.7	20.3	60.0

continued

Table A 9 continued

	1965-1970			1952-1961			1961-1970		
	IS	EE	DD	IS	EE	DD	IS	EE	DD
Electrical energy	- 2.6	8.6	94.0	13.6	4.1	82.3	- 5.8	12.4	93.4
Coal and coke	-38.9	26.8	112.1	8.9	10.0	81.1	9.2	15.0	75.8
Crude petroleum	- .02	4.0	96.0	41.0	5.3	53.7	- 1.9	6.6	95.3
Ferrous metals	-68.0	30.1	137.9	22.0	15.6	62.4	-11.2	25.1	86.1
Non-ferrous metals	-45.0	54.3	90.7	- 7.6	6.9	100.7	- 9.5	48.3	61.2
Non-metallic minerals	-43.8	17.9	125.9	.3	23.7	76.0	- 9.5	22.1	87.4
Metal products	-21.6	7.2	114.4	20.3	10.0	69.7	15.9	9.9	74.2
Shipbuilding	-16.0	47.3	68.7	- 4.8	25.9	78.9	-16.6	62.6	54.0
Electrical machinery, etc.	- 1.4	13.0	88.4	48.2	8.5	43.3	19.5	13.3	67.2
Chemicals	-14.3	15.8	98.5	19.3	8.5	72.2	16.7	15.2	68.1
Building materials	- 7.2	3.4	103.8	11.5	2.0	86.5	- 2.6	3.8	98.8
Wood products	-10.7	12.4	98.3	- 1.1	22.2	78.9	- 4.5	16.3	88.2
Paper and paper products	-34.7	18.7	116.0	14.4	12.0	73.6	- 5.0	21.0	84.0
Textiles	2.4	21.2	76.4	-13.7	21.9	91.8	22.2	17.1	60.7
Leather and footwear	-36.2	39.0	97.2	18.4	17.7	63.9	-22.7	42.1	80.6
Rubber	- 2.6	10.8	91.8	30.8	2.2	67.0	10.9	10.2	78.9
Food products	2.6	4.6	92.8	24.3	7.8	67.9	7.6	5.1	87.3
Printing, publishing	3.0	2.3	94.7	13.3	1.2	85.5	2.5	2.6	94.9
Tobacco manufactures	-14.1	-14.1	128.2	0	13.7	83.3	- 3.9	39.5	64.4
Motion pictures	- 7.8	17.0	90.8	- 9.5	3.8	105.7	- 7.6	0	107.6
Total[b]	-16.1	15.9	100.2	7.2	14.3	78.5	5.2	17.9	76.9

[a]Based on current price data. - Source of growth attributed to import substitution ≡ IS, to export expansion ≡ EE, to domestic demand ≡ DD. - [b]Weighted average (gross output weights).

Source: SZzS [Statistički godišnjak SFRJ, various years]. - SZzS [Statistika spoljne trgovine SFRJ, various years]. - SZzS [Medjusobni odnosi privrednih delatnosti SFRJ, 1962, 1966]. - Exchange rates used to obtain direct export and import values: 7.50 dinars per US $ for 1952-1956, 1956-1961, 1952-1961 (1962 input-output table used in these periods); 12.50 dinars for the remaining periods (1966 input-output table used in these periods). See text for method of calculation.

Table A 10 - Employment and Unemployment, 1952-1974

Year	Paid employment[a]	Industrial employment[a]	Registered unemployment[b]	Unemployment as percent of paid employment plus registered unemployment
	1,000			
1952	1,721	562	44.7	2.5
1953	1,824	592	81.6	4.3
1954	1,994	691	76.2	3.7
1955	2,213	748	67.2	2.9
1956	2,216	788	99.3	4.3
1957	2,392	856	115.9	4.6
1958	2,552	929	132.0	4.9
1959	2,730	991	161.6	5.6
1960	2,972	1,072	159.2	5.1
1961	3,242	1,128	191.3	5.6
1962	3,318	1,165	236.6	6.7
1963	3,390	1,222	230.2	6.4
1964	3,608	1,319	212.5	5.6
1965	3,662	1,378	237.0	6.1
1966	3,582	1,358	257.6	6.7
1967	3,561	1,352	291.5	7.0
1968	3,587	1,349	311.0	8.0
1969	3,706	1,398	330.6	8.2
1970	3,850	1,454	319.6	7.7
1971	4,034	1,531	291.3	6.7
1972	4,210	1,614	315.3	7.0
1973	4,306	1,665	381.6	8.1
1974	4,514	1,757	448.7	9.0

[a]Average of March and September totals. - [b]Average of monthly totals.

Source: SZzS [Statistički godišnjak SFRJ 1974, Tables 104.1, 104.15, 109.1; 1968, Tables 104.1, 104.14; 1963, Table 104.1; 1962, Table 203.6]. - SZzS [Jugoslavija 1945-1964, Tables 4.1, 4.13]. - SZzS [Indeks, Vol. 24, 1975, No. 4, pp. 39 sq.].

Table A 11 - Yugoslav Emigrant Workers, 1954-1971

Year	Estimated number of Yugoslav emigrant workers in Europe	Year	Estimated number of Yugoslav emigrant workers in Europe
1954	3,000	1963	90,000
1955	3,500	1964	115,000
1956	4,000	1965	140,000
1957	4,500	1966	210,000
1958	10,000	1967	220,000
1959	15,000	1968	230,000
1960	18,000	1969	420,000
1961	30,000	1970	550,000
1962	50,000	1971	660,000

Source: Baučić [1972, p. 3].

Table A 12 - Structure of Exports and Imports by SITC Sections, 1952-1973 (in current value)

SITC	Description	1952	1953	1954	1955	1956	1957	1958	1959	1960	1961	1962	1963	1964	1965	1966	1967	1968	1969	1970	1971	1972	1973
		percent of total exports																					
	Structure of exports																						
0	Food and live animals	38.2	18.4	29.7	23.5	25.7	24.7	29.5	26.4	28.9	29.7	23.3	25.4	23.7	21.2	20.4	22.8	17.3	16.7	15.2	14.2	14.9	14.0
1	Beverages and tobacco	4.0	3.8	4.3	7.7	8.1	6.8	8.6	4.9	4.7	3.9	4.3	4.9	5.6	4.5	3.9	4.1	3.3	2.9	3.5	3.4	2.6	2.1
2	Crude material, inedible, except fuels	26.2	37.7	29.7	29.3	23.7	20.8	16.9	15.9	15.7	14.8	13.8	14.2	13.2	10.1	8.8	8.5	10.0	9.7	9.4	8.2	8.2	9.6
3	Mineral fuels, etc.	1.6	1.2	1.3	1.0	1.3	1.6	1.3	1.0	.9	1.2	2.5	2.0	1.4	1.0	1.7	1.8	1.0	1.0	1.2	1.1	.8	.8
4	Animal and vegetable oils and fats	.0	.0	.0	.0	.0	.0	.0	.0	.2	.0	.1	.0	.0	.0	.0	.2	.2	.2	.1	.2	.1	.1
5	Chemicals	4.0	5.3	4.4	5.5	4.5	4.9	3.3	3.3	4.0	3.6	3.1	3.2	4.2	5.5	5.7	5.9	6.1	6.2	5.8	7.1	6.4	6.2
6	Manufactured goods classified by material	24.4	29.4	24.8	27.5	27.6	27.3	23.1	24.9	23.7	22.8	22.7	21.4	22.9	22.7	23.2	22.4	25.6	29.2	29.3	27.2	27.0	28.5
7	Machinery and transport equipment	.0	1.6	3.4	1.8	4.6	6.8	10.7	17.4	15.0	16.5	22.8	19.5	17.0	23.5	24.6	20.3	21.9	20.4	22.7	24.5	24.4	24.7
8	Miscellaneous manufactured articles	.6	1.6	1.9	2.8	3.6	5.5	5.6	6.1	6.8	7.4	7.3	9.2	11.8	11.5	11.7	13.9	14.6	13.7	12.7	14.0	15.2	13.4
9	n.e.s.	1.0	1.1	.5	.9	.9	1.6	1.0	.1	.1	.1	.1	.2	.2	.0	.0	.1	.0	.0	.1	.1	.5	.6
0-4[a]	Primary commodities	69.9	61.1	65.0	61.5	58.8	53.9	56.3	48.2	50.4	49.6	44.0	46.5	43.9	36.8	34.8	37.4	31.8	30.5	29.4	27.1	26.6	26.6
5-8[a]	Manufactured goods	29.1	37.9	34.5	37.6	40.3	44.5	42.7	51.7	49.5	50.3	55.9	53.3	55.9	63.2	65.2	62.5	68.2	69.5	70.5	72.8	73.0	72.9
		percent of total imports																					
	Structure of imports																						
0	Food and live animals	21.8	28.2	24.3	27.5	31.8	22.2	19.1	19.3	9.2	13.2	14.3	18.4	12.6	14.7	14.7	10.2	6.9	6.6	7.0	8.9	9.3	11.1
1	Beverages and tobacco	.0	.0	.0	.3	.0	.2	.0	.0	.0	.1	.4	.7	.2	.0	.4	.4	.2	.3	.2	.2	.2	.2
2	Crude material, inedible, except fuels	13.9	12.7	15.0	17.6	15.9	14.7	12.3	14.0	14.3	14.3	14.9	15.0	15.8	16.8	13.5	11.7	11.0	12.4	10.9	9.6	10.4	10.8
3	Mineral fuels, etc.	7.8	7.8	8.8	8.3	9.9	9.9	6.0	6.6	5.4	4.4	5.4	4.4	5.0	5.6	5.2	5.0	5.5	4.9	4.8	5.9	5.5	7.9
4	Animal and vegetable oils and fats	1.2	1.3	1.8	1.2	1.2	2.0	2.1	2.3	1.4	1.7	1.6	1.0	1.1	1.0	.6	1.8	1.1	.3	.7	1.5	1.3	0.5
5	Chemicals	4.7	4.4	6.1	6.7	7.0	7.3	9.8	10.9	8.6	7.0	8.8	10.5	10.4	9.2	9.5	9.8	10.5	10.3	9.3	9.1	10.8	10.0
6	Manufactured goods classified by material	17.7	12.7	15.2	11.5	12.2	15.7	15.8	15.7	20.8	20.3	18.4	17.7	21.0	21.7	23.5	23.5	23.8	25.5	28.8	28.2	26.1	24.0
7	Machinery and transport equipment	31.4	31.8	26.8	25.3	19.9	25.3	31.5	27.9	36.9	35.6	33.1	29.0	30.1	27.6	29.1	33.5	35.9	33.2	33.3	31.3	31.5	31.4
8	Miscellaneous manufactured articles	1.5	1.3	1.7	1.6	2.1	2.2	3.0	3.0	3.3	3.4	3.1	3.2	3.8	3.4	3.5	4.1	5.1	5.8	5.0	5.2	4.7	4.1
9	n.e.s.	.0	.0	.1	.1	.0	.5	.4	.3	.1	.0	.0	.0	.0	.0	.0	.0	.0	.0	.0	.1	.2	.2
0-4[a]	Primary commodities	44.7	49.9	49.9	54.9	58.8	49.0	39.5	42.2	30.3	33.7	36.6	39.5	34.7	38.1	34.4	29.1	24.7	24.5	23.6	26.1	26.7	30.5
5-8[a]	Manufactured goods	55.3	50.1	49.8	45.1	41.2	50.5	60.1	57.5	69.6	66.3	63.4	60.4	65.3	61.9	65.6	70.9	75.3	74.8	76.4	73.8	73.1	69.4

[a] Totals may not add to 100 because of errors due to rounding.

Source: SZzS [Statistika spoljne trgovine SFRJ, various years].

Table A 13 - Structure of Exports and Imports by Use of Products and Stage of Production, 1939, 1946-1973 (percent)

Year	Use of products						Stage of production					
	raw materials and semi-manufactures		capital goods		consumer goods		raw materials		semi-finished goods		finished goods	
	exports	imports	exports	imports	exports	imports	exports	imports	exports	imports	exports	imports
1939	78	49	-	28	22	23	55	20	39	26	6	54
1946	62	74	-	5	38	21	44	36	33	29	23	35
1947	67	73	-	18	33	9	45	31	39	24	16	45
1948	50	73	-	17	50	10	50	22	35	33	15	45
1949	64	72	-	20	36	8	48	26	46	29	7	45
1950	70	73	-	20	30	7	43	31	50	25	7	44
1951	77	53	-	16	23	31	34	31	58	35	8	34
1952	56	65	-	25	44	10	50	28	43	25	7	46
1953	68	45	1	26	31	29	33	38	50	18	17	44
1954	57	52	3	22	40	26	38	39	46	21	17	41
1955	61	51	1	20	37	29	38	42	46	18	16	40
1956	54	51	3	14	43	35	37	45	43	19	21	36
1957	53	55	4	18	44	27	32	36	42	23	27	41
1958	44	52	8	24	48	24	35	26	36	25	30	49
1959	47	56	12	20	41	24	26	31	37	23	37	47
1960	46	57	10	29	45	15	26	20	39	23	36	57
1961	44	52	11	28	46	20	25	24	38	22	37	54
1962	44	54	18	25	39	21	20	27	37	22	43	51
1963	42	58	14	20	44	22	21	30	37	22	43	48
1964	42	63	12	22	46	16	17	24	39	25	44	52
1965	42	62	17	20	41	18	13	28	31	23	54	49
1966	43	58	18	22	39	21	13	25	33	23	53	53
1967	48	57	14	22	38	21	16	18	3[illegible]	25	53	57
1968	50	57	16	25	35	18	14	16	3[illegible]	23	54	62
1969	53	60	14	22	34	18	13	17	34	23	53	60
1970	52	63	14	21	33	15	12	15	34	27	54	59
1971	50	64	15	21	35	15	11	17	32	27	57	57
1972	51	63	14	21	35	16	12	16	31	25	57	59
1973	53	62	14	22	33	16	9	18	35	25	57	57

Source: SZzS [Jugoslavija 1945-1964]. - SZzS [Statistika spoljne trgovine SFRJ, various years].

Table A 14 - Gross Turnover, Fixed Assets, Employment, Capital/Output, Labor/Output and Capital/Labor Ratios, 1968

Sector	Gross turnover	Fixed assets (actual value)	Employment (annual average)	Capital/output ratio					
				100,000 new dinars per million new dinars of output		rank (sec. 1-29)		rank (sec. 1-20)	
	million new dinars		number	direct	cumulative	direct	cumulative	direct	cumulative
1. Electrical energy	6,645	13,923	37,849	20.9526	25.4453	2	5	1	4
2. Coal and coke	2,621	2,847	68,635	10.8623	17.7612	6	9	3	6
3. Crude petroleum	4,087	2,318	18,746	5.5716	14.4746	10	11	7	8
4. Ferrous metals	4,327	3,594	48,712	8.306	27.5290	8	4	5	3
5. Non-ferrous metals	4,966	3,261	51,795	6.5667	22.2294	9	8	6	5
6. Non-metallic minerals	1,795	1,044	42,558	5.8162	13.4773	11	15	8	12
7. Metal products	15,160	5,349	251,072	3.5284	14.3009	17	12	11	9
8. Shipbuilding	2,123	689	21,404	3.2454	14.2997	20	13	13	10
9. Electrical machinery, apparatus, appliances and supplies	6,476	1,504	84,502	2.7857	14.2354	24	14	17	11
10. Chemicals	7,052	3,679	70,818	5.2170	16.0378	13	10	10	7
11. Building materials	2,484	1,390	52,174	5.5958	12.5622	12	18	9	14
12. Wood products	5,436	4,680	129,338	8.6093	28.0001	7	3	4	2
13. Paper and paper products	2,231	2,699	27,120	12.0977	26.9264	5	2	2	1
14. Textiles	10,810	3,788	217,231	3.5042	11.6488	18	20	12	16
15. Leather and footwear	2,678	485	41,172	1.8111	9.6663	28	25	20	19
16. Rubber products	1,435	407	23,935	2.8362	11.2142	23	22	16	18
17. Food products	10,045	3,156	88,720	3.1419	11.3350	21	21	14	17
18. Printing and publishing	3,187	906	47,838	2.8428	12.8955	22	16	15	13
19. Tobacco manufactures	2,197	474	17,763	2.1575	11.7187	26	19	18	15
20. Motion pictures	242	44	1,139	1.8182	5.4631	27	27	19	20
21. Miscellaneous manufacturing industries	301	77	5,299	2.5581	12.8540	25	17		
22. Agriculture	38,238	18,053	4,540,000	4.7212	9.2726	14	26		
23. Forestry	2,064	10,270	63,242	49.7576	52.8718	1	1		
24. Construction	17,103	2,664	309,674	1.5576	10.6565	29	23		
25. Transport and communications	14,908	28,055	299,248	18.8188	23.6399	4	6		
26. Trade and catering	26,461	9,895	374,779	3.7395	5.3277	16	28		
27. Service rendering arts and crafts	7,039	2,690	369,000	3.8216	10.1823	15	24		
28. Public utilities	1,471	2,902	27,705	19.7281	23.8947	3	7		
29. Scrap and waste	586	196	10,093	3.3447	3.3447	19	29		

continued

Table A 14 continued

Sector	Labor/output ratio: tens of man-years per million new dinars of output		rank (sec. 1-29)		rank (sec. 1-20)		K/L	K^*/L^{*a}	Rank K/L		Rank K^*/L^*		Index[b] of K^*/L^*
	direct	cumulative	direct	cumulative	direct	cumulative			sec. 1-29	sec. 1-20	sec. 1-29	sec. 1-20	
1. Electrical energy	.5696	1.5575	27	28	18	19	36.7848	16.3373	1	1	1	1	331
2. Coal and coke	2.6187	3.8479	4	15	1	10	4.1480	4.6158	10	7	11	8	93
3. Crude petroleum	.4587	1.7126	29	27	20	18	12.8005	8.4513	3	2	5	3	171
4. Ferrous metals	1.1258	4.3121	21	9	12	6	7.3775	6.3840	7	4	7	4	129
5. Non-ferrous metals	1.0430	3.6354	22	18	13	13	6.2960	6.1147	8	5	8	5	124
6. Non-metallic minerals	2.3709	3.9122	6	12	3	8	2.4532	3.4449	18	14	18	15	70
7. Metal products	1.6561	3.8926	15	14	7	9	2.1305	3.6739	20	16	16	13	74
8. Shipbuilding	1.0082	3.5394	23	19	14	14	3.2190	4.0396	14	11	13	10	52
9. Electrical machinery, apparatus, appliances and supplies	1.3048	3.7590	19	17	16	12	2.1350	3.7870	19	15	15	12	77
10. Chemicals	1.0042	3.3239	24	21	15	16	5.1952	4.9512	9	6	10	7	100
11. Building materials	2.1004	3.4256	7	20	4	15	2.6642	3.6672	16	13	17	14	44
12. Wood products	2.3793	4.9628	5	7	2	5	3.6184	5.6420	12	9	9	6	114
13. Paper and paper products	1.2156	3.9257	20	11	11	7	9.9520	9.4063	5	3	3	2	190
14. Textiles	2.0095	7.4585	8	5	5	4	1.7438	1.5618	23	18	25	18	32
15. Leather and footwear	1.5374	7.9534	16	4	8	3	1.1780	1.2154	26	20	27	19	25
16. Rubber products	1.6679	3.8094	14	16	6	11	1.7005	2.9438	24	19	20	16	60
17. Food products	.8832	9.4501	25	3	16	2	3.5574	1.9995	13	10	23	17	40
18. Printing and publishing	1.5010	2.9923	17	23	9	17	1.8929	4.3096	22	17	12	9	87
19. Tobacco manufactures	.8085	9.6740	26	2	17	1	2.6685	1.2114	15	12	28	20	25
20. Motion pictures	.4707	1.4391	28	29	19	20	3.8628	3.7962	11	8	14	11	77
21. Miscellaneous manufacturing industries	1.7605	4.8700	12	8			1.4531	2.6394	25		22		
22. Agriculture	11.7945	17.7038	1	1			.4089	.5233	29		29		
23. Forestry	3.0641	3.9077	3	13			16.2340	13.5302	2		2		
24. Construction	1.8106	4.0246	11	10			.8603	2.6478	27		21		
25. Transport and communications	2.0073	3.1463	9	22			9.3752	7.6407	6		6		
26. Trade and catering	1.4163	1.8037	18	25			2.6403	2.9538	17		19		
27. Service rendering arts and crafts	5.2422	6.9731	2	6			.7290	1.4592	28		26		
28. Public utilities	1.8834	2.6406	10	24			10.4747	9.0496	4		4		
29. Scrap and waste	1.7224	1.7224	13	26			1.9419	1.9419	21		24		

[a] K^*/L^* = cumulative capital/labor ratio. - [b] Weighted average = 4.9388 = 100.

Source: SZzS [Medjusobni odnosi privrednih delatnosti SFRJ 1968]. - SZzS [Statistički godišnjak SFRJ 1970, pp. 104, 120 sq.]. - Yugoslav Survey [Vol. 11, 1970, No. 2, p. 53]. - Inputs of scrap and waste estimated.

Table A 15 - Total Capital and Labor Requirements of Yugoslav Exports and Imports, 1968

	Total capital requirements of exports	Total labor requirements of exports	Total capital requirements of imports	Total labor requirements of imports
	100,000 new dinars	tens of man-years	100,000 new dinars	tens of man-years
Electrical energy	107.02	65.51	997.30	610.43
Coal and coke	184.16	398.99	5,984.71	12,965.72
Crude petroleum	2,109.41	2,495.89	16,265.30	19,245.38
Ferrous metals	9,960.02	15,601.44	43,334.53	67,879.48
Non-ferrous metals	37,172.11	60,792.01	22,988.20	37,595.36
Non-metallic minerals	4,193.23	14,262.23	8,200,60	23,804.88
Metal products	28,661.63	78,014.06	129,729.17	353,109.65
Shipbuilding	22,279.53	55,152.28	6,110.57	15,126.51
Electrical machinery, etc.	16,586.55	43,798.09	25,146.61	66,401.60
Chemicals	17,555.87	35,458.54	49,568.27	100,115.68
Building materials	1,317.91	3,593.81	1,560.65	4,255.74
Wood products	40,201.76	71,253.77	4,045.15	7,169.64
Paper and paper products	15,352.08	16,321.02	13,411.30	14,257.75
Textiles	20,026.90	128,228.49	18,994.43	121,617.79
Leather and footwear	8,724.27	71,783.28	1,907.53	15,695.14
Rubber products	625.67	2,125.40	4,364.47	14,825.96
Food products	9,964.43	83,073.62	10,019.70	83,534.40
Printing and publishing	425.63	987.64	1,359.35	3,154.28
Tobacco manufactures	3,712.92	30,650.87	120.96	998.55
Motion pictures	82.87	218.30	52.61	138.59
Miscellaneous manufactures	1,009.41	3,824.35	3,190.41	12,087.49
Agriculture	22,719.14	433,768.09	4,121.36	432,764.28
Forestry	10,638.86	7,863.03	4,635.27	3,425.86
Construction	3,000.06	11,330.27	-	-
Transport and communications	79,770.54	104,402.95	11,030.01	14,435.98
Trade and catering	11,498.54	38,927.80	1,152.54	3,901.88
Service rendering arts and crafts	289.84	1,986.30	-	-
Public utilities	-	-	-	-
Scrap and waste	169.78	874.32	357.44	1,840.71
Total	368,340.14	1,317,252.35	384,648.44	1,430,958.73

Source: Table A 14. - SZzS [Statistika spoljne trgovine SFRJ 1969].

Table A 16 - Ranking of Industrial Branches According to Skill Intensity, 1968

Industry branch	Wage value-added per employee		Personnel with secondary education and above, highly skilled and skilled	
	new dinars	rank	percent of employees	rank
Electrical energy	16, 090	4	63. 7	2
Coal and coke	9, 674	16	41. 0	13
Crude petroleum	17, 897	2	62. 6	3
Ferrous metals	10, 800	9	48. 6	6
Non-ferrous metals	12, 754	6	45. 2	9
Non-metallic minerals	9, 028	18	33. 8	17
Metal products	10, 722	11	51. 6	5
Shipbuilding	15, 208	5	58. 8	4
Electrical machinery, etc.	11, 273	8	46. 0	8
Chemicals	12, 229	7	44. 3	10
Building materials	10, 032	13	30. 3	20
Wood products	8, 354	19	33. 4	18
Paper and paper products	9, 904	15	38. 0	15
Textiles	7, 933	20	32. 9	19
Leather and footwear	9, 254	17	42. 8	11
Rubber products	9, 935	14	41. 7	12
Food products	10, 745	10	39. 5	14
Printing, etc.	16, 476	3	47. 2	7
Tobacco manufactures	10, 060	12	35. 4	16
Motion pictures	58, 999	1	65. 0	1
Total industry	10, 612		46. 8	

Source: Calculated from data in: SZzS [Statistički godišnjak SFRJ 1970, Table 106. 6]. - SZzS [Industrijska preduzeća 1968, Table 4; 1970, Table 6].

Table A 17 - Yugoslav Exports and Imports by Convertible and Bilateral Areas, 1966-1973 (million US $)

Year	Convertible currency area			East-European bilateral account countries			Other bilateral account countries		
	exports	imports	balance	exports	imports	balance	exports	imports	balance
1966	622	768	- 146	449	415	34	149	130	19
1967	677	1, 113	- 436	455	459	- 4	120	136	-16
1968	693	1, 177	- 484	436	489	- 53	134	131	3
1969	882	1, 456	- 574	455	508	- 53	138	170	-32
1970	1, 013	2, 149	-1, 136	551	593	- 42	115	132	-17
1971	1, 058	2, 330	-1, 272	670	778	-108	86	144	-58
1972	1, 381	2, 348	- 967	792	797	- 5	64	88	-24
1973	1, 895	3, 350	-1, 455	868	1, 020	-152	90	141	-51

Source: National Bank of Yugoslavia [1974, Tables 20, 21].

Table A 18 - Foreign Investment in the Industrial Sector - Disaggregated[a], January 31, 1974

Industries	Total joint venture (domestic plus foreign share)	Foreign partner share		Structure of foreign investment
	1,000 US $		percent	
Crude petroleum and natural gas	10,675	5,231	49.0	4.1
Iron works	244,830	5,278	2.2	4.2
Non-ferrous metals	34,738	3,386	9.7	2.7
Glass factories	99	40	40.4	b
Ceramic and porcelain	9,380	3,855	41.1	3.0
Road vehicles	202,548	48,221	23.8	38.0
Railroad vehicles	844	355	42.1	.3
Reproduction materials	24,403	7,043	28.9	5.6
Machinery and accessories	18,469	3,055	16.5	2.4
Precision instruments	1,957	465	23.8	.4
Electrical machinery	50,277	4,315	8.6	3.4
Cables	1,467	715	48.7	.6
Electrical supplies	6,000	2,833	46.7	2.2
Other electrical appliances	185	90	48.6	.1
Basic chemicals	47,217	12,797	27.1	10.1
Chemicals and products	1,969	554	28.1	.4
Medicaments	14,436	5,940	40.5	4.7
Artificial matter	3,558	1,685	47.4	1.3
Chemicals - unclassified	995	472	47.4	.4
Stone quarries and lime kilns	129	45	34.9	b
Other building materials	559	200	35.8	.2
Finished wood articles	3,348	837	25.0	.7
Paper processing and factories	41,168	6,494	15.0	5.1
Under and outer wear	204	100	49.0	.1
Other textiles	99	48	48.5	b
Other spinning and weaving	923	452	49.0	.4
Textiles - unclassified	1,189	589	49.5	.5
Rubber products	31,654	10,459	33.0	8.2
Canned food	6,894	879	12.8	.7
Starch and similar products	1,231	209	17.0	.2
Printing works	250	123	49.2	.1
Cigarettes	290	116	40.0	.1
Total	761,985	126,881	16.7	100[c]

[a]Twelve joint ventures are excluded from this list because they are not in the industrial sector or classification was not possible. - [b]Less than .1. - [c]May not add to 100 due to rounding.

Source: Compiled from data in OECD [Foreign Investment 1974, pp. 38-65].

Bibliography

Books and Articles

Ahmad, Jaleel, "Import Substitution and Structural Change in Indian Manufacturing Industry, 1950-1966", The Journal of Development Studies, Vol. 4, London, 1968, pp. 352-379.

Anakioski, Dušan, "Foreign Trade in the Years of the Reform", Yugoslav Survey, Vol. 10, Belgrade, 1969, No. 3, pp. 71-84.

Avsenek, Ivan, "Basic Industries", in: Robert F. Byrnes (Ed.), Yugoslavia, New York, 1957, pp. 282-309.

Bajit, Aleksander, "Yugoslav Economic Reforms, Monetary and Production Mechanism", Economics of Plannung, Vol. 7, Oslo, 1967, No. 3, pp. 201-218.

--, "Instability with Planning", in: Michael Kaser, Richard Portes (Eds.), Planning and Market Relations, London, New York, 1971, pp. 64-79.

Balassa, Bela A., "Trade Liberalization and 'Revealed' Comparative Advantage", The Manchester School of Economic and Social Studies, Vol. 33, Manchester, 1965, pp. 99-123.

Baldwin, Robert E., "Determinants of the Commodity Structure of U.S. Trade", The American Economic Review, Vol. 61, Menasha, Wisc., 1971, pp. 126-146.

Banerji, Ranadev, "Major Determinants of the Share of Manufactured Exports: A Cross-Section Analysis and Case Study of India", Weltwirtschaftliches Archiv, Vol. 108, Tübingen, 1972, pp. 345-381.

--, "The Export Performance of Less-Developed Countries: A Constant Market Share Analysis", ibid., Vol. 110, 1974, pp. 447-481.

Baučić, Ivo, The Effects of Emigration from Yugoslavia and the Problems of Returning Emigrant Workers, The Hague, 1972.

Behrman, Jack N., "State Trading by Undeveloped Countries", Law and Contemporary Problems, Vol. 24, Durham, N.C., 1959, No. 3, pp. 455-481.

Bhagwati, Jagdish N., Anne O. Krueger, "Exchange Control, Liberalization, and Economic Development", The American Economic Review, Vol. 63, Menasha, Wisc., 1973, Papers and Proceedings, pp. 419-427.

Bićanić, Rudolf, "Economics of Socialism in a Developed Country", Foreign Affairs, Vol. 44, New York, 1966, No. 4, pp. 633-650. Also appears in: Idem, Turning Points in Economic Development, The Hague, 1972, as "Economics of Socialism in Yugoslavia: The Third Stage - The Reform".

--, Economic Policy in Socialist Yugoslavia, Cambridge, 1973.

Bildner, R., Strategies and Effects of Multinational Corporations in Iran and Yugoslavia, Scholar of the House Essay, Yale University, New Haven, Conn., 1973.

Blumenthal, Tuvia, "Exports and Economic Growth: The Case of Postwar Japan", The Quarterly Journal of Economics, Vol. 86, Cambridge, Mass., 1972, pp. 617-631.

Bombelles, Joseph T., Economic Development of Communist Yugoslavia, 1947-1964, Stanford, Calif., 1968.

Bruton, Henry J., "The Import-Substitution Strategy of Economic Development. A Survey", The Pakistan Development Review, Vol. 10, Karachi, 1970, No. 2, pp. 123-146.

Byrnes, Robert F. (Ed.), Yugoslavia, New York, 1957.

Chenery, Hollis B., "Patterns of Industrial Growth", The American Economic Review, Vol. 50, Menasha, Wisc., 1960, pp. 324-354.

--, Shuntaro Shishido, Tsunehiko Watanabe, "The Pattern of Japanese Growth, 1914-1954", Econometrica, Vol. 30, New Haven, Conn., 1962, pp. 98-129.

Chittle, Charles R., "Symmetry between Total Imports and Exports", Problemi spoljne trgovine i konjunkture, Vol. 13, Belgrade, 1974, No. 3, pp. 239-245.

--, (1975a): "Direct Foreign Investment in a Socialist Labor-Managed Economy - The Yugoslav Experience", Weltwirtschaftliches Archiv, Vol. 111, Tübingen, 1975, pp. 770-784.

--, (1975b): "Jugoslawiens Industriewarenexporte: Politik, Ergebnisse und Perspektiven", Die Weltwirtschaft, Tübingen, 1975, 1, pp. 48-68.

Crawford, J.T., "Yugoslavia's New Economic Strategy: A Progress Report", in: United States Congress, Joint Economic Committee, Economic Developments in Countries of Eastern Europe, Washington, D.C., 1970, pp. 608-634.

Dimitrijević, Dimitrije, George Macesich, Money and Finance in Contemporary Yugoslavia, London, New York, 1973.

Dirlam, Joel B., James L. Plummer, An Introduction to the Yugoslav Economy, Columbus, Ohio, 1973.

Domandžić, Ante, "Customs Tariffs", Yugoslav Survey, Vol. 7, Belgrade, 1966, No. 24, pp. 3485-3488.

Domar, Evsey D., "On Collective Farms and Producer Cooperatives", The American Economic Review, Vol. 56, Menasha, Wisc., 1966, pp. 734-757.

Donges, Juergen B., "Die Entwicklungsländer als Anbieter industrieller Erzeugnisse", Die Weltwirtschaft, Tübingen, 1971, 1, pp. 41-61.

--, "Shaping Spain's Export Industry: Experience, Problems, Prospects", World Development, Vol. 1, Oxford, 1973, No. 9, pp. 19-37.

--, James Riedel, The Expansion of Manufactured Exports in Developing Countries: An Empirical Assessment of Supply and Demand Issues, Institut für Weltwirtschaft, Kiel Working Papers, 49, Kiel, June 1976.

Dunning, John Harry, "The Determinants of International Production", Oxford Economic Papers, N.S., Vol. 25, Oxford, 1973, pp. 289-336.

Dyker, David A., "The Yugoslav Deficit on Balance of Payments", European Economic Review, Vol. 5, Amsterdam, 1974, pp. 329-354.

Džeba, Krešo, Milan Beslać, Privredna Reforma, Zagreb, 1965.

Ekonomska Politika, Vol. 23, Belgrade, November 11, 1974, pp. 17-22.

Ellsworth, Paul T., J. Clark Leith, The International Economy, 5th Ed., London, New York, 1975.

Fabinc, Ivo, "Review of V. Pertot, Ekonomik medjunarodne razmjene Jugoslavije", Vol. 2, Zagreb, 1970, in: International Problems, Vol. 13, Belgrade, 1972, pp. 154-163.

Fane, George, "Import Substitution and Export Expansion: Their Measurement and an Example of Their Application", The Pakistan Development Review, Vol. 11, Karachi, 1971, pp. 1-17.

--, "Consistent Measures of Import Substitution", Oxford Economic Papers, N.S., Vol. 25, Oxford, 1973, pp. 251-261.

Fels, Gerhard, Klaus-Werner Schatz, Frank Wolter, "Der Zusammenhang zwischen Produktionsstruktur und Entwicklungsniveau, Versuch einer Strukturprognose für die westdeutsche Wirtschaft", Weltwirtschaftliches Archiv, Vol. 106, Tübingen, 1971 I, pp. 240-278.

Frković, Mirko, "Disparitet spoljnotrgovinskih kurseva u našoj privredi", Ekonomist, Vol. 10, Belgrade, 1957, pp. 79-97.

Furubotn, Eirik G., "Toward a Dynamic Model of the Yugoslav Firm", The Canadian Journal of Economics, Vol. 4, Toronto, 1971, pp. 182-197.

--, "The Long-Run Analysis of the Labor-Managed Firm: An Alternative Interpretation", The American Economic Review, Vol. 66, Menasha, Wisc., 1976, pp. 104-123.

--, Svetozar Pejovich, "Property Rights, Economic Decentralization, and the Evolution of the Yugoslav Firm, 1965-1972", The Journal of Law and Economics, Vol. 16, Chicago, Ill., 1973, pp. 275-302.

Giersch, Herbert (Ed.), The International Division of Labour - Problems and Perspectives, International Symposium, Tübingen, 1974.

Girgis, Maurice A., "Determinanten der industriellen Entwicklung in Ägypten, 1950 bis 1970", Die Weltwirtschaft, Tübingen, 1973, 1, pp. 113-140.

Gorupić, Drago, Ivan Paj, Workers' Self-Management in Yugoslav Undertakings, Ekonomski Institut, Zagreb, 1970.

Hamilton, F.E. Ian, Yugoslavia, Patterns of Economic Activity, London, 1968.

Hartz, Clyde D., "A Business Trip to Eastern Europe: Joint Ventures and Practical Lessons", Business Economics, Vol. 9, Washington, D.C., 1974, No. 4, pp. 34-40.

Healey, Derek T., "Development Policy: New Thinking about an Interpretation", Journal of Economic Literature, Vol. 10, Menasha, Wisc., 1972, pp. 757-797.

Heckscher, Eli F., "The Effects of Foreign Trade on the Distribution of Income", Ekonomisk Tidskrift, Vol. 31, Stockholm, 1919, pp. 497-512, Repr. in: Howard S. Ellis, L. Metzler (Eds.), Readings in the Theory of International Trade, Homewood, Ill., 1949, pp. 272-300.

Helleiner, Gerald K., "Manufactured Exports from Less-Developed Countries and Multinational Firms", The Economic Journal, Vol. 83, London, 1973, No. 329, pp. 21-47.

Hirschman, Albert O., National Power and the Structure of Foreign Trade, Berkeley, Los Angeles, 1945.

--, The Strategy of Economic Development, Yale Studies in Economics, 10, New Haven, Conn., 1958.

Hoffman, George W., Fred Warner Neal, Yugoslavia and the New Communism, New York, 1962.

Holt, John B., "Joint Ventures in Yugoslavia: West German and American Experience", Michigan State University Business Topics, Vol. 21, East Lansing, 1973, No. 2, pp. 51-63.

Horvat, Branko, "Prilog zasnivanju teorije jugoslavenskog poduzeća", Ekonomska analiza, Vol. 1, Belgrade, 1967, No. 1-2, pp. 8-28.

--, "Yugoslav Economic Policy in the Post-War Period: Problems, Ideas, Institutional Developments", The American Economic Review, Vol. 61, Menasha, Wisc., 1971, No. 3, Suppl., pp. 69-169.

Huddle, Donald L., "Postwar Brazilian Industrialization: Growth Patterns, Inflation, and Sources of Stagnation", in: Eric N. Baklanoff (Ed.), The Shaping of Modern Brazil, Baton Rouge, La., 1969, pp. 86-108.

Jančić, L., "The New External Trade and Foreign Exchange System", Yugoslav Survey, Vol. 8, Belgrade, 1967, No. 4, pp. 91-96.

Jovanovic, Mihalo, "Yugoslav Trade with EEC and COMECON Countries", Law and Contemporary Problems, Vol. 37, Durham, N.C., 1972, pp. 586-591.

Kayser, Bernard, Cyclically-Determined Homeward Flows of Migrant Workers, and the Effects of Emigration, OECD, Paris, 1972.

Keesing, Donald B., "Labor Skills and International Trade", The Review of Economics and Statistics, Vol. 47, Cambridge, Mass., 1965, pp. 287-294.

Keesing, Donald B., "Labor Skills and Comparative Advantage", The American Economic Review, Vol. 56, Menasha, Wisc., 1966, Papers and Proceedings, pp. 249-258.

--, "Outward-looking Policies and Economic Development", The Economic Journal, Vol. 77, London, 1967, pp. 303-320.

Kerner, Robert Joseph (Ed.), Yugoslavia, Berkeley, Los Angeles, London, 1949.

Kidrič, Boris, "Economic Problems of the FNRY", Belgrade, 1946, quoted in: Dimitrije Mišić, "Policy of Industrialization of the SFR Yugoslavia", in: Socialism in Yugoslav Theory and Practice, University International Center for Social Sciences of the University of Belgrade, 7th Session, Belgrade, 1965.

Komunist, Belgrade, August 19, 1974.

Kovač, Oskar, "Yugoslavia's Balance of Payments Policy", International Problems, Vol. 14, Belgrade, 1973, pp. 5-30.

Kramer, Jane, "The Invandrare", New Yorker, New York, March 22, 1976, pp. 43-85.

Kuznets, Simon, "Quantitative Aspects of the Economic Growth of Nations: IX. Level and Structure of Foreign Trade, Comparisons for Recent Years", Economic Development and Cultural Change, Vol. 13, Chicago, Ill., 1964, No. 1, P. II.

Lary, Hal B., Imports of Manufactures from Less-Developed Countries, National Bureau of Economic Research, Studies in International Economic Relations, 4, London, New York, 1968.

Leamer, Edward E., Robert M. Stern, Quantitative International Economics, Boston, 1970.

Leontief, Wassily, "Domestic Production and Foreign Trade: The American Capital Position Re-Examined", Proceedings of the American Philosophical Society, Vol. 97, Philadelphia, Pa., 1953, No. 4, pp. 332-349.

Lewis, Stephen R., Ronald Soligo, "Growth and Structural Change in Pakistan Manufacturing Industry, 1954-1964", The Pakistan Development Review, Vol. 5, Karachi, 1965, pp. 94-139.

Little, Ian, Tibor Scitovsky, Maurice Scott, Industry and Trade in Some Developing Countries: A Comparative Study, London, New York, Toronto, 1970.

Macesich, George, "Major Trends in the Postwar Economy of Yugoslavia", in: W. Vucinich (Ed.), Contemporary Yugoslavia, Berkeley, Los Angeles, 1969, pp. 203-235.

Madžar, Ljubomir, "Jedna empirijska analiza stabilnosti spoljnotrgovinskih tokova", Ekonomist, Vol. 21, Belgrade, 1968, pp. 580-587.

Madžić, Slobodan, "Certain Issues Related to Yugoslavia's Trade with the COMECON Countries", International Problems, Vol. 10, Belgrade, 1969, pp. 101-112.

Maizels, Alfred, Industrial Growth and World Trade, National Institute of Economic and Social Research, Economic and Social Studies, 21, Cambridge, Mass., 1963.

--, Growth and Trade, Being an Abbreviated Version of Industrial Growth and World Trade, Cambridge, Mass., 1970.

Maurice, S. Charles, C.E. Ferguson, "Factor Usage by a Labour-Managed Firm in a Socialist Economy", Economica, N.S., Vol. 39, London, 1972, No. 153, pp. 18-31.

Mase-Lago, Carmelo, "Unemployment in a Socialist Economy: Yugoslavia", Industrial Relations, Vol. 10, Berkeley, Calif., 1971, No. 1, pp. 49-69.

Michaely, Michael, Concentration in International Trade, Amsterdam, 1962.

Milenkovitch, Deborah D., Plan and Market in Yugoslav Economic Thought, New Haven, Conn., London, 1971.

Morawetz, David, "Employment Implications of Industrialisation in Developing Countries: A Survey", The Economic Journal, Vol. 84, London, 1974, pp. 491-542.

Morley, Samuel A., Gordon W. Smith, "On the Measurement of Import Substitution", The American Economic Review, Vol. 60, Menasha, Wisc., 1970, pp. 728-735.

Müller-Ohlsen, Lotte, "Möglichkeiten und Grenzen des Industriegüterexports der Türkei", Die Weltwirtschaft, Tübingen, 1975, 1, pp. 114-138.

Mujahid, Ghazy B.S., "Industrialisierung und Expansion der Fertigwarenausfuhr in Pakistan. Unter besonderer Berücksichtigung der wirtschaftlichen Verflechtung mit Bangladesch", Die Weltwirtschaft, Tübingen, 1975, 1, pp. 80-99.

Neuberger, Egon, "General Survey of the Yugoslav Economy", in: Robert F. Byrnes (Ed.), Yugoslavia, New York, 1957, pp. 192-210.

--, "Legacies of Central Planning", in: Alan A. Brown, Egon Neuberger (Eds.), International Trade and Central Planning, Berkeley, Los Angeles, 1968, pp. 349-383.

Nikolin, Zoran, "Some Basic Features of Yugoslavia's Industrial Development in 1952-1972", Yugoslav Survey, Vol. 14, Belgrade, 1973, No. 3, pp. 155-162.

Obradović, Josip, "Workers' Participation: Who Participates?", Industrial Relations, Vol. 14, Berkeley, Calif., 1975, No. 1, pp. 32-44.

Ohlin, Bertil, Interregional and International Trade, Harvard Economic Studies, Vol. 39, Rev. Ed., Cambridge, Mass., London, 1967.

Pertot, Vladimir, Yugoslavia's Foreign Trade, Jugoslavija, Belgrade, 1958.

--, "Yugoslavia's Economic Relations with Eastern European Countries", Co-existence, Vol. 4, Oxford, 1967, pp. 7-13.

--, Ekonomika medjunarodne razmjene Jugoslavije, Vol. 2, Dokumentacija, Zagreb, 1970.

--, "Long-Term Tendencies in Development of the Yugoslav Balance of Payments", International Problems, Vol. 12, Belgrade, 1971, pp. 33-53.

Plummer, James L., "Inter-Firm Production Function Analysis of Yugoslav Industrial Resource Allocation", The Journal of Industrial Economics, Vol. 19, Oxford, 1970, pp. 66-81.

Pomfret, Richard W.T., (1975a): "Die Industrieexporte Israels: Bisherige Entwicklung und Zukunftsaussichten", Die Weltwirtschaft, Tübingen, 1975, 1, pp. 25-47.

--, (1975b): "Some Interrelationships between Import Substitution and Export Promotion in a Small Economy", Weltwirtschaftliches Archiv, Vol. 111, Tübingen, 1975, pp. 714-727.

--, Trade Policies and Industrialization in a Small Country: The Case of Israel, Kieler Studien, 141, Tübingen, 1976.

R a d o v a n o v i ć , Milija, "Joint Investment by Domestic Enterprises and Business and Financial Cooperation between Yugoslav and Foreign Firms", Yugoslav Survey, Vol. 9, Belgrade, 1968, No. 1, pp. 43-50.

R a s m u s s e n , P. Nørregaard, Studies in Inter-Sectoral Relations, Amsterdam, 1956.

R i c h a r d s o n , J. David, "Constant-Market-Shares Analysis of Export Growth", Journal of International Economics, Vol. 1, Amsterdam 1971, pp. 227-239.

R i e d e l , James, (1975a): "The Nature and Determinants of Export-Oriented Direct Foreign Investment in a Developing Country: A Case Study of Taiwan", Weltwirtschaftliches Archiv, Vol. 111, Tübingen, 1975, pp. 505-528

--, (1975b): "Wirtschaftspolitik und Exportentwicklung in Taiwan", Die Weltwirtschaft, Tübingen, 1975, 1, pp. 100-113.

--, "A Balanced-Growth Version of the Linkage Hypothesis: A Comment", The Quarterly Journal of Economics, Vol. 90, Cambridge, Mass., 1976, pp. 319-322.

R o c k w e l l , Charles S., The Relevance of Illyria for Less Developed Countries, Yale University, Economic Growth Center, Center Discussion Paper, No. 56, New Haven, Conn., June 1968.

S a c k s , Stephen R., Entry of New Competitors in Yugoslav Market Socialism, University of California, Institute of International Studies, Research Series, No. 19, Berkeley, Calif., 1973.

S e k u l i ć , Mijo, "Osjetljivost Jugoslavenske privrede na promjene uvoznih cijena, strukturna analiza", Ekonomski pregled, Vol. 23, Zagreb, 1972, No. 3-4, pp. 131-146.

S t e c h e r , Bernd, Erfolgsbedingungen der Importsubstitution und der Exportdiversifizierung im Industrialisierungsprozeß - Die Erfahrungen in Chile, Mexiko und Südkorea, Kieler Studien, 136, Tübingen, 1976.

S t e u e r , Max David, Constantin S. V o i v o d a s , "Import Substitution and Chenery's Patterns of Industrial Growth: A Further Study", Economia Internazionale, Vol. 18, Genova, 1965, pp. 47-82.

S t r e e t e n , Paul P. (Ed.), Trade Strategies for Development, London 1973.

S u k i j a s o v i ć , Miodrag, Yugoslav Foreign Investment Legislation at Work: Experiences so Far, 2. Ed., Belgrade, New York, 1970.

--, (1973a): "Investment of Foreign Capital in the Yugoslav Economy", Yugoslav Survey, Vol. 14, Belgrade, 1973, No. 4, pp. 41-54.

--, (1973b): Joint Business Ventures in Yugoslavia between Domestic and Foreign Firms: Developments in Law and Practice, Belgrade, Luxembourg, 1973.

T o m a s e v i c h , Jozo, "Foreign Economic Relations, 1918-1941", in: Robert J. K e r n e r (Ed.), Yugoslavia, Berkeley, Los Angeles, London, 1949, pp. 169-214.

T r a v i s , William P., The Theory of Trade and Protection, Harvard Economic Studies, Vol. 121, Cambridge, Mass., 1964.

T r p u t e c , Zoran, "Economic Development and Foreign Trade Diversification - The Experience of Underdeveloped Countries and the Case of Yugoslavia", Medjunarodni poroblemi, Vol. 24, Belgrade, 1972, No. 2, Repr. in: International Problems, Vol. 14, Belgrade, 1973, pp. 117-127.

T y l e r , William G., Methodological Notes on Analyzing the Manufactured Export Performance in Less Developed Countries, Institut für Weltwirtschaft, Kiel Discussion Papers, 28, Kiel, February 1973.

--, Manufactured Export Expansion and Industrialization in Brazil, Kieler Studien, 134, Tübingen, 1976.

T y s o n , Laura, "Liquidity Crises in the Yugoslav Economy: An Alternative to Bankruptcy?", Soviet Studies, Vol. 29, Glasgow, 1977, No. 2, pp. 284-295.

T y s z i n s k i , H., "World Trade in Manufactured Commodities, 1899-1950", The Manchester School of Economic and Social Studies, Vol. 19, Manchester, 1951, pp. 272-304.

V a n e k , Jaroslav, The General Theory of Labor-Managed Market Economies, Ithaca, London, 1970.

--, "The Yugoslav Economy Viewed Through the Theory of Labor Management", World Development, Vol. 1, Oxford, 1973, No. 9, pp. 39-56.

V e r n o n , Raymond, "International Investment and International Trade in the Product Cycle", The Quarterly Journal of Economics, Vol. 80, Cambridge, Mass., 1966, pp. 190-207.

Vratusa, Antun, "Jugoslavia, 1971", Foreign Affairs, Vol. 50, New York, 1971, No. 1, pp. 148-162.

Vucinich, Wayne S., "Interwar Yugoslavia", in: Idem (Ed.), Contemporary Yugoslavia, Berkeley, Los Angeles, 1969, pp. 3-58.

Wachtel, Howard M., Workers' Management and Workers' Wages in Yugoslavia", Ithaca, London, 1973.

Ward, Benjamin, "The Firm Illyria: Market Syndicalism", The American Economic Review, Vol. 48, Menasha, Wisc., 1958, pp. 566-589.

--, The Socialist Economy, A Study of Organizational Alternatives, New York, 1967.

Wogart, Jan Peter, "Erfahrungen mit der exportorientierten Industrialisierungsstrategie in Kolumbien", Die Weltwirtschaft, Tübingen, 1975, 1, pp. 69-79.

Yotopoulos, Pan A., Jeffrey B. Nugent, "A Balanced-Growth Version of the Linkage Hypothesis: A Test", The Quarterly Journal of Economics, Vol. 87, Cambridge, Mass., 1973, pp. 151-171.

Yugoslav Survey, Belgrade:

"Changes in Yugoslav Foreign Trade and Foreign Exchange System", Vol. 2, 1961, No. 5, pp. 673-680.

"The Customs System", Vol. 4, 1963, No. 14, pp. 2042-2050.

"Platform for the Preparation of Positions and Decisions of the Tenth Congress of the League of Communists of Yugoslavia", Vol. 14, 1973, No. 3, pp. 1-140.

"The System and Organization of Foreign Trade", Vol. 4, 1963, No. 14, pp. 2029-2041.

Official Publications and Statistical Sources

The Constitution of the Socialist Federal Republic of Yugoslavia (Dopisna Delavska Univerza), Ljubljana, 1974.

Ekonomski Institut, Efektivna carinska zaštita v Jugoslavije, Ljubljana, 1971.

Ekonomski Institut FNRJ, Privreda FNRJ u 1952 Godini, Belgrade.

Institut za ekonomisku investicija, Investicije 1947-1969, Belgrade, 1971.

International Monetary Fund (IMF), Annual Report on Exchange Restrictions, Washington, D.C., various issues.

National Bank of Yugoslavia, Quarterly Bulletin, Vol. 2, Belgrade, 1974, No. 3.

Organisation for Economic Co-operation and Development (OECD):

Economic Survey of Yugoslavia, Paris, various issues.

Foreign Investment in Yugoslavia, Paris, 1974.

Trade by Commodities, Series B, Paris, various years.

Official Gazette of the Socialist Federal Republic of Yugoslavia, Belgrade, various issues.

Pick's Currency Yearbook, New York, various issues.

Savezni Zavod za Statistiku (SZzS):

Indeks, Belgrade, various issues.

Industrija 1973, Statistički Bilten, Belgrade.

Industrijska preduzeća, 1968, 1970, Statistički Bilten, Belgrade.

Jugoslavija 1945-1964, Statistički pregled, Belgrade, 1965.

Medjusobni odnosi privrednih delatnosti SFR Jugoslavije - Uvoz po delatnostima porekla i namene, Belgrade, various years.

O radu carinske službe za 1971 Godište, Statistički Bilten, Belgrade.

Statistički godišnjak SFR Jugoslavije, Belgrade, various years.

Statistika spoljne trgovine SFR Jugoslavije, Belgrade, various years.

United Nations (UN):

Economic Bulletin for Europe, New York, various years.

Handbook of International Trade and Development Statistics, UN Publ. E/F. 72. II. D. 3., New York, 1972.

Monthly Bulletin of Statistics, New York, September 1974.

Statistical Yearbook 1956, New York.

Yearbook of International Trade Statistics, New York, various years.

UN, Conference on Trade and Development (UNCTAD):

(1964a): Methods and Experiences of Promoting Exports of Manufactured Goods in Yugoslavia, Geneva, 1964.

(1964b): Towards a New Trade Policy for Development: Report by the Secretary General, Raul Prebish, New York, 1964.

World Bank Country Economic Report, Yugoslavia: Development with Decentralization, Baltimore, London, 1975.

Yugoslav Life, Vol. 20, Belgrade, 1975, No. 8-9.

Yugoslav Survey, Belgrade, various issues.

Kieler Studien

Institut für Weltwirtschaft an der Universität Kiel

Herausgegeben von Herbert Giersch
Schriftleitung: Hubertus Müller-Groeling

134. William G. Tyler, Manufactured Export Expansion and Industrialization in Brazil. 1976. XXIII, 373 S. Broschiert *DM* 78,–. Leinen *DM* 88,–.
135. Jürgen Roth, Der internationale Konjunkturzusammenhang bei flexiblen Wechselkursen. Eine modelltheoretische Analyse. 1975. XII, 264 S. Broschiert *DM* 54,–. Leinen *DM* 64,–.
136. Bernd Stecher, Erfolgsbedingungen der Importsubstitution und der Exportdiversifizierung im Industrialisierungsprozeß. Die Erfahrungen in Chile, Mexiko und Südkorea. 1976. XI, 207 S. Broschiert *DM* 43,–. Leinen *DM* 53,–.
137. Hugo Dicke, Hans H. Glismann, Ernst-Jürgen Horn, Axel D. Neu, Beschäftigungswirkungen einer verstärkten Arbeitsteilung zwischen der Bundesrepublik und den Entwicklungsländern. 1976. XVI, 225 S. Broschiert *DM* 42,–. Leinen *DM* 52,–.
138. Peter Trapp, Geldmenge, Ausgaben und Preisanstieg in der Bundesrepublik Deutschland. 1976. XI, 229 S. Broschiert *DM* 42,–. Leinen *DM* 52,–.
139. Ernst-Jürgen Horn, Technologische Neuerungen und internationale Arbeitsteilung. Die Bundesrepublik Deutschland im internationalen Vergleich. 1976. XIX, 382 S. Broschiert *DM* 68,–. Leinen *DM* 78,–.
140. Klaus Möbius, Ekkehart Seusing, Adolf Ahnefeld, Die Pharmazeutische Industrie in der Bundesrepublik Deutschland. Struktur und Wettbewerb. 1976. XIII, 139 S. Broschiert *DM* 34,–. Leinen *DM* 46,–.
141. Richard W. T. Pomfret, Trade Policies and Industrialization in a Small Country: The Case of Israel. 1976. XVI, 204 S. Broschiert *DM* 42,–. Leinen *DM* 52,–.
142. Wolf-Dieter Zumpfort, Untersuchungen zum Wachstum des Eurodollarmarktes. 1977. XVII, 175 S. Broschiert *DM* 39,–. Leinen *DM* 49,–.
143. Maurice Girgis, Industrialization and Trade Patterns in Egypt. Im Druck.
144. Hugo Dicke, Die Wirkungen strukturpolitischer Maßnahmen in der Ernährungsindustrie. Analyse und Prognose. 1977. XV, 230 S. Broschiert *DM* 46,–. Leinen *DM* 56,–.
145. Charles R. Chittle, Industrialization and Manufactured Export Expansion in a Worker-Managed Economy. The Yugoslav Experience. 1977. XIV, 168 S. Broschiert *DM* 36,–. Leinen *DM* 46,–.
146. Dieter Biehl, Günter Hagemann, Karl H. Jüttemeier, Harald Legler, Konjunkturelle Wirkungen öffentlicher Haushalte. In Vorbereitung.
147. Klaus Stegemann, Price Competition and Output Adjustment in the European Steel Market. Im Druck.
148. Seev Hirsch, Rich Man's, Poor Man's, and Every Man's Goods. Aspects of Industrialization. Im Druck.
149. Hilde Wander, Bevölkerungswachstum und Konsumstruktur in Entwicklungsländern. Fakten, Zusammenhänge und politische Implikationen. 1977. XII, 117 S. Broschiert *DM* 28,–. Leinen *DM* 38,–.

J. C. B. Mohr (Paul Siebeck) Tübingen
Postfach 2040, D-7400 Tübingen
ISSN 0340 - 6989